PARENTS CARRY A FULL CREDIT LOAD, TOO

PARENTS AND STUDENTS:

THE PARTNERSHIP FOR
SUCCESS IN COLLEGE

Richard M. Oxhandler
Associate Professor
Western Michigan University
Kalamazoo, MI 49008

KENDALL/HUNT PUBLISHING COMPANY
2460 Kerper Boulevard P.O. Box 539 Dubuque, Iowa 52004-0539

TABLE OF CONTENTS

CHAPTER FOUR - LONELINESS

CHAPTER FIVE - STRESS MANAGEMENT

CHAPTER SIX - SELF-CONCEPT

CHAPTER SEVEN - FEAR AND RISK-TAKING

CHAPTER EIGHT - SEX-ROLE STEREOTYPES

CHAPTER NINE - RELATIONSHIPS

CHAPTER TEN - LEARNING STYLES

CHAPTER ELEVEN - DECISION MAKING

CHAPTER TWELVE - TOLERANCE, ACCEPTANCE AND SOCIOMETRY

CHAPTER THIRTEEN - KALAMAZOO

CHAPTER FOURTEEN - TERMINATION

PARENTS CARRY A FULL CREDIT LOAD, TOO

INTRODUCTION

Dear Parents:

You picked up this book for a reason. Is it that your first child is preparing to leave for college? Your second, or third? Are you just curious about what would be in a book for the parents of college students? Whatever the reason, this book can help you help your children to be successful in college. It will enable you to understand what your son or daughter will be experiencing in college and to effectively work with them to make the college experience more rewarding-for them and for you! However, there are no magical solutions offered in this book. For you to benefit most you will have to put energy into examining the content presented, observing your sons and daughters going through the growth process, and honestly evaluating your attitudes, values, beliefs, and behaviors to determine how they may be impacting on your child's growth and happiness. Considering that college costs thousands of dollars per year, your investment in this book will result in a return many times greater than your initial outlay if you do just one or two things to help your child be more successful in school.

On its own this book is of limited value. But when utilized with understanding, commitment, consistency and caring, it can be a valuable resource to you as you work to support your child's efforts to make his or her dreams a reality during one of the most exciting periods of their lives-their college years.

Why is this book written to parents if it is the children who have to do the actual work to be successful in college? Why not write to them? Good questions. I have written a book for students called *Expanding Perceptual Boundaries*. This text is intended to help students be successful in all arenas of their college lives by addressing many issues too often ignored in classes and other texts. It can give them a solid understanding and appreciation of the many attributes required to be a well-rounded and successful person. It will provide them with a growth process they can use the rest of their lives, and encourage them to believe in themselves, others, and all they can accomplish.

At Western Michigan University we have used the *Expanding Perceptual Boundaries* text in our UNIV 101 course. Students who have taken this course had statistically significantly higher grade point averages and retention rates than students who did not take the course. Students were more successful on these measures as well as perceiving themselves to be more confident in their ability to successfully deal with the challenges of college, more willing to take risks to grow, more satisfied with their first year of college, and more self-confident.

All right, back to why a book for parents? There is a simple reason which involves several parts. Fundamentally, it is because you love and care about your children and want them to be happy and successful. The parent-child relationship is the most influential relationship in our lives; no other relationship has the special characteristics, longevity, complexity, or potential for growth. Parents can exert a positive influence on their sons and daughters which will contribute to their child's success in college yet few colleges and few parents know how to consistently and caringly provide the necessary support once the child becomes a college student. During my more than eighteen years in higher education as an administrator, teacher, and counselor, I have heard many students express a desire to have their parents involved in a positive way in their educational pursuits; a way that respects the growing independence and responsibility of a young adult.

It is a challenge for parents who aren't on the college scene to know what is going on and, therefore, must rely on communications from their sons and daughters. Ineffective communication has been a strain on or has led to a breakdown in the relationship between too many parents and children. There are many reasons for the difficulty parents and children have in communicating in helpful ways which will be addressed in the book. For now, recognize that in general your child wants to be able to discuss many issues and decisions they face with you to get your ideas and input and sometimes your understanding, sympathy, and support. Often students have been unsure of how to make sense of what they have been experiencing and, therefore, have been very frustrated trying to explain their problems to parents. That is another reason why the *Expanding Perceptual Boundaries* book was written for students; to help them to understand, to explain more clearly, and to learn from their experiences.

This book, *Parents Carry a Full Credit Load, Too,* will serve as a valuable bridge for parents wishing to understand and constructively work with their son or daughter. To maximize your effectiveness with your son or daughter, it would be best to read this book during their first term of college since this time period is particularly stressful. It is also a time when many parents feel uncertain about how much influence they should have. This is a normal concern and guidelines will be provided to aid you in this delicate balancing task. As you may be guessing by now, your role as a parent is far from over. But it is taking a very important new direction; one which can potentially benefit you as parents and your child as they develop into a mature young adult. This book will provide you with several useful structures to serve as reference points as you work with your son or daughter. There is too much "content" to memorize and that is not necessary if you utilize structures like the *Success Triad* and *Expanding Perceptual Boundaries growth model*. In addition, there are guidelines for showing caring and love that may surprise some people. For ultimately, this book is a book of love because the attitudes, beliefs, values, and behaviors necessary to help your child grow and be successful are love in action.

ORGANIZATION OF THIS BOOK

This book is organized to facilitate your understanding of the issues facing your daughter or son in college and to enhance your ability to work effectively with them. Chapter titles are identical to those in the *Expanding Perceptual Boundaries* text used by students and though the content is nearly the same, it has been altered to be appropriate for you the parent reader. By making these two books parallel in content and organization, you can **work together in a caring and supportive partnership** with your son or daughter.

There are some important differences between this book and the ***Expanding Perceptual Boundaries*** text. In ***Parents Carry a Full Credit Load, Too,*** the *Success Triad* (Figure 1) is introduced. Simply, the *Success Triad* represents the need for the right amounts of *challenge, support, and caring* if optimal success is to be obtained. You will understand the nature of the *challenges* before your son or daughter as a student and yourself as a parent, the material, time, skill, and other *supports* necessary for success in meeting the challenges, and the *caring* attitudes and behaviors that can optimize performance on and add the deepest sense of personal satisfaction and fulfillment in meeting the challenges.

In addition to the EPB Mind Stretchers in the text for your child, this book adds six Mind Stretchers for you. The purpose is to interest you in thinking in different ways about the material covered in the chapter and to give you a first hand knowledge of the process being utilized in the EPB text to facilitate the advancement of critical thinking skills in your daughter or son.

The fourteen chapters of this book are organized in a developmental sequence because students will, in general, experience the challenges of each chapter in a sequential fashion. For example, they make the transition from home to college first and later, approximately week four, begin to experience significant consequences of their loneliness. Since the book also contains the expanding perceptual boundaries process for growth, certain skills, attitudes, knowledge, and behaviors tend to build from one chapter to the next. Therefore, to best understand what your child is experiencing, read the chapters in sequence. However, if a particular issue is pressing or just of interest it will probably be of most value to your child and you to address that chapter as needed and then return to the next chapter in sequence.

By picking up this book, you have shown a commitment to helping your son or daughter be a more successful and happy person. I firmly believe that you will succeed. Best wishes.

SUCCESS TRIAD

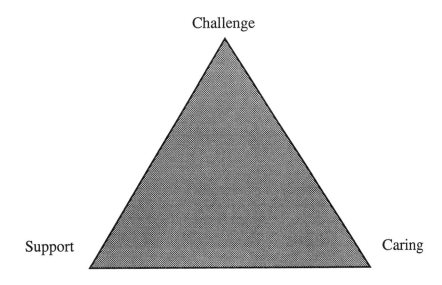

Figure 1

ACKNOWLEDGMENTS

Through their ideas, beliefs, activities, or personal behavior, many people have contributed to this book.

I wish to acknowledge my colleagues at Western Michigan University's Counseling Center whose encouragement, suggestions, and energy over many years of courses and workshops helped shape the content and purpose of this book. In particular, I wish to acknowledge Diann Miller and Moyra Ebling for their dedication to students, solid ideas, and courage to teach UNIV 101, a 'new course' which was the impetus for *EXPANDING PERCEPTUAL BOUNDARIES.* Chuck Spaniolo and Karen Schaaf made valuable editorial comments. June Mochizuki contributed many helpful activities as well as encouraged me to do workshops and courses over the years which gave me the material and confidence to write this book.

I also wish to acknowledge Sue Esman and Evelyn Freemire for their typing, proofreading and editing, and Betty Roberts for her work on diagrams and tables. Rick Wedeking's expertise on the computer and encouragement have been invaluable and sincerely appreciated. I wish to acknowledge the faculty, students, and administrators who sat on committees that authorized the teaching of UNIV 101 which eventually led me to write this book.

I wish to thank Jerie Wood, psychologist, and Bob Knerr, friend and outdoor adventure educator, who helped me to integrate the theories, techniques, and beliefs of many learned theorists, writers, and practitioners, and contributed greatly to my personal growth. To Jerie, who is also my wife and best friend, goes my love and thanks for believing in me and this text and helping me to expand more boundaries than I could have imagined.

I especially want to acknowledge the contributions of thousands of students in classes, workshops, or counseling sessions from whom I have learned so much about life. Their sharing of their joys and sorrows, failures and successes is a valued gift.

Parents of college students deserve much thanks. It was their love, caring, and desire to help their children be successful and happy that convinced me of the need for this book.

Chapter One
Transition

EXPANDING PERCEPTUAL BOUNDARIES

Imagine having had pictures taken of your child each and every day of his or her life. These pictures would not only reveal their physical appearance, but also the breadth and depth of their innermost thoughts and feelings. If such a camera existed and had taken such pictures, what do you think would be revealed to your discerning eye? Look closely. You're beginning to see some patterns, aren't you?

Your child's pattern is unique to them. Nobody else on earth has exactly the same pattern. Yet, as human beings, we all have some common trends. The first trend is that although we can see our life as a whole unit, we tend to compartmentalize it into the physical, academic, social, personal, career, spiritual, family, and sexual arenas. The second trend is that each of these arenas can expand or contract. The third trend is that expansion is most rapid early in life, and contraction is most likely later in life. (Figure 2)

Let's see how these trends apply to the patterns you were identifying in your child's life. If you look at the physical arena, you will notice tremendous growth from birth to the present. Your son or daughter is taller, wider, heavier, and stronger than they were at birth, and they are also capable of performing more complex physical movements. Some of your greatest joys came from watching your child change and grow. The physical limitations of an infant are not the limitations of a young adult. In other words, their physical boundaries have expanded over the years.

EPB CHART

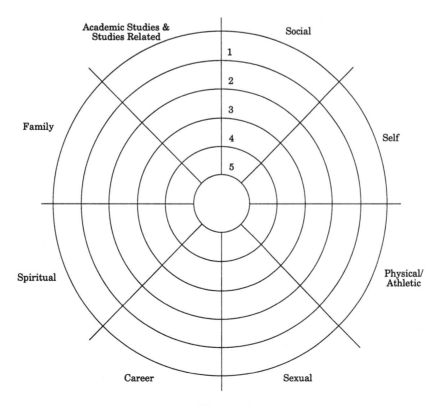

Figure 2

2

Now look at their intellectual arena. Here, again, you will notice the trend of rapid growth in terms of the amount of information known and the mental processes used to manipulate the information. The reason many students are in college is to greatly expand their boundaries in the intellectual arena.

There were times, however, when their perceptions of their boundaries or limitations have been inaccurate. Perhaps they thought that they would never be able to do the required number of sit-ups for the physical fitness test at school, but they did them all! Or they were the one who was not good at math, yet managed to get a 'B' in the course! Or they never thought that one of the school's brightest and best looking students could ever be interested in them but the following Saturday they went out on their first date together! Remember as a parent what it was like being part of their lives as they started dating! Do you remember when your perceptions of your son or daughter were accurate and when they weren't?

Perceptions are funny sometimes. They may be accurate, slightly inaccurate, or very inaccurate. Whatever their accuracy they are very important because they are the basis for all our behaviors. Your behavior is based on your perception of yourself, others, and your situation and so is your child's behavior. And it is their behaviors that will result in their success in college. Your accurate perception of their behaviors and capacities will enable you to provide the appropriate parental support necessary to help your child be more successful than they would be without such support.

Success will be somewhat different for each of our children as students. Generally most students identify progress toward academic and career goals, having friends, maintaining a healthy lifestyle, having favorable family relationships, and having a general sense of satisfaction with self necessary to consider themselves successful.

In order to achieve their definition of success, many behaviors involving numerous skills or competencies and based on constructive attitudes, beliefs, and values will be required. Since no course or text book can **GIVE** your child all the content necessary to develop the behaviors needed for success, this book wants to **EMPOWER YOU** as a parent with enough content to understand the major developmental and situational issues facing your daughter or son and a process for supporting the success of your child. Once you understand how to utilize the **process of expanding perceptual boundaries** to support the success of your child in college you may decide to use it to be more successful in your own life. How can we expend the energy, effort, commitment, and love necessary to help our children without it enriching the quality of our own lives!

THE GREAT TRANSITION

As an entering college student your son or daughter has just begun the greatest transition of their life, the transition from home and dependence to college and eventual independence. They have, no doubt, already found that this change has resulted in mood swings, a kaleidoscope of emotions. One minute they may be elated over having made a new friend or intellectually excited by a stimulating lecture and the next, they may be overwhelmed by the amount of work required for classes or lonely because the people (parents, brothers, sisters) they love most are far away. These feelings are natural and will tend to be less disconcerting as they go about answering these two very important questions. Who am I? Where do I fit?

All of us human beings try to answer these questions every time we are placed in a new situation with new people. Who you are and where you fit has been, in a large part, a product of the people and environment at home. Because home for most of them now is many miles away, they must establish new reference points. (Figure 3)

Keep in mind that no one at WMU knows who they were or where they fit back home. This presents them with an exciting opportunity. They can work to preserve the best parts of themselves and drop the parts they don't like, as well as expand their definition of themselves in new and exciting ways. All of our children, no matter how effective or ineffective our parenting skills, know there are things about themselves which they value and wish to nourish and have grow and things they wish to let go of and replace with new, more functional and healthful attitudes, beliefs, or behaviors. This book will serve as a guide for you to better understand and support their quest.

Please remember that what you get out of this book is mostly your responsibility. A good start is to be open and honest in your communications with your daughter or son and in your assessment of yourself as a parent and of your child as a young adult. Next, if you commit yourself to doing what is in the best interest of your child and devote the necessary time and energy, then your relationship with your son or daughter will grow. The trust, respect, understanding, and love between you will deepen. It is these somewhat intangible qualities that are so essential if your daughter or son is to take the risks necessary to expand their perceptual boundaries and to grow as a competent, caring, and loving individual.

WMU Student Transition from High School to WMU in Terms of Support Groups

Figure 3

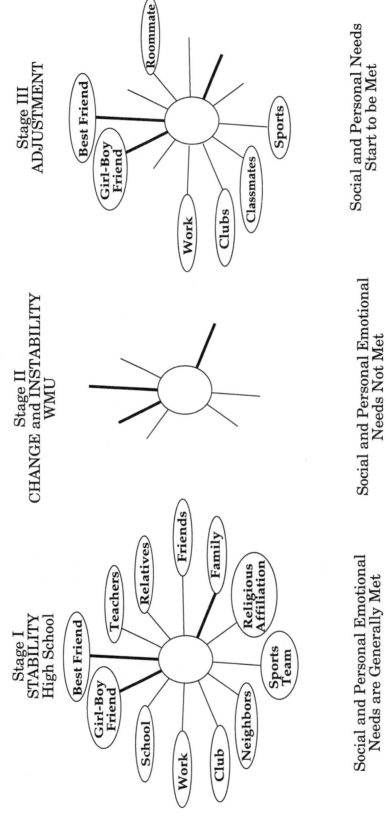

Stage I
STABILITY
High School

Best Friend
Girl-Boy Friend
Teachers
Relatives
Friends
Family
School
Work
Club
Neighbors
Sports Team
Religious Affiliation

Stage II
CHANGE and INSTABILITY
WMU

Stage III
ADJUSTMENT

Roommate
Best Friend
Girl-Boy Friend
Work
Clubs
Classmates
Sports

Social and Personal Emotional Needs are Generally Met

Loneliness Minimal

Social and Personal Emotional Needs Not Met

Maximum Loneliness

Social and Personal Needs Start to be Met

Loneliness Decreasing

———— Strong Emotional Ties

———— Social Ties

EPB ASSESSMENT

The Risk-Taking Behavior in Groups and the Life-Space Situations questionnaires that follow are an aid to help you more clearly identify with your son's or daughter's perceptual boundaries. The items that comprise the two questionnaires have particular relevance to them as first year students.

Once you have completed the questionnaires and the accompanying EPB worksheets, you will have a visual map showing your child's arenas of greatest fear and least competence and those arenas of their greatest confidence and most competence. By the end of the Fall semester they will notice significant expansion of many of their boundaries.

Just imagine what that expansion will be by the time they graduate from Western! This expansion is growth and growth is at the heart of education and of life.

RISK-TAKING BEHAVIOR IN GROUPS QUESTIONNAIRE*

Risk-taking behavior in groups is one way your child has of expanding boundaries to obtain personal growth goals. Risk-taking is behavior that ordinarily one would not engage in, that a person would see as posing a possible threat to her/himself. What constitutes a risk for a person depends on whether it is new behavior and whether he/she has a subjective sense of danger involved in the behavior.

Creative risk-taking in groups can be an effective way to increase the variety of responses you have to different interpersonal situations. With a greater variety of responses available to you, you gain a greater freedom of choice, unrestricted by inhibitions. You have a greater spontaneity of action and more flexibility in your interpersonal relationships. Your chances for growth and happiness are enhanced.

The purpose of this questionnaire is to ascertain what you perceive your child would consider risky behavior for him or her in a group situation. Another purpose is to stimulate your thinking with regard to the risk-taking your child may engage in to help them grow.

Read the statements on the following pages and rate them with regard to how much subjective risk you believe your son or daughter would feel when involved in this behavior. Use as a reference a group you have seen them with and one which to the best of your guesses approximates the group they are spending time with now in college. In front of each item, write the appropriate number from the scale at the top of the page.

When you have completed this exercise your EPB Worksheet will be similar to the example shown in Figure 4.

Adapted from Pfeiffer and Jones, Structured Experiences for Human Relations Training.

Risk-Taking Behavior in Groups Questionnaire

1	Would be no risk for her/him.
2	Would be a small risk for him/her.
3	I have no feelings one way or the other, or I don't know
4	Would be some risk for her/him.
5	Would be a high risk for him/her.

EPB
Arena

Self	___	1.	Disclosing certain negative feelings about myself to others.
Self	___	2.	Revealing certain things about my past to others.
Self	___	3.	Asking for help with my problems from others.
Soc	___	4.	Expressing anger toward someone in the group.
Soc	___	5.	Expressing affection toward someone in the group.
Soc	___	6.	Receiving affection from someone in the group.
Soc	___	7.	Asking for feedback from significant members in the group.
Phy	___	8.	Touching someone else in the group.
Soc	___	9.	Having someone else touch me in the group.
Soc	___	10.	Becoming close and personal with another in front of the group.
Soc	___	11.	Making a statement which might anger someone else in the group.
Soc	___	12.	Expressing and dealing with conflict I have with another member in the group.
Soc	___	13.	Giving another member negative feedback.
Self	___	14.	Being the center of attention in the group.
Self	___	15.	Expressing my confusion and uncertainty in front of the other group members.
Soc	___	16.	Expressing anger or dissatisfaction with the group leader.
Soc	___	17.	Admitting that I was wrong about some other person in the group.
Soc	___	18.	Admitting to the group that I was wrong about an idea that I had.

EPB
Arena

Sex	___	19.	Talking about sexual feelings in the group.
Soc	___	20.	Sharing a fantasy I have about some member or the total group.
Soc	___	21.	Telling someone in the group that they have become very important to me.
Soc	___	22.	Expressing indifference toward other group members.
Soc	___	23.	Expressing feelings about another member's physical characteristics.
Self	___	24.	Talking about my feelings with regard to my physical characteristics.
Soc	___	25.	Admitting that someone had hurt my feelings in the group.
Soc	___	26.	Telling the group members to leave me alone, to "get off my back".
Soc	___	27.	Walking out of the group while under stress.
Sex	___	28.	Expressing sexual attraction toward another member in the group.

Enter the risk level number (1-5) you selected for each item (1-28) on the EPB worksheet on the following page. For example, if you rated item #14, 'Being the center of attention in the group', at the #3 risk level, you would put the #14 in the Self arena at level #3.

Transfer your responses to the Risk-Taking in Groups Summary Sheet, page 183.

Figure 4

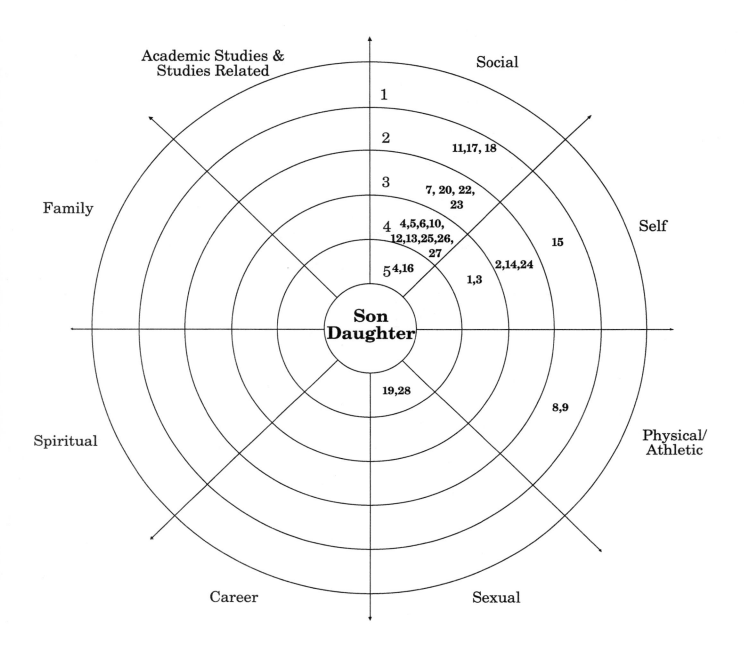

EPB Worksheet - Example
Risk-Taking In Groups

EPB Worksheet
Risk-Taking in Groups

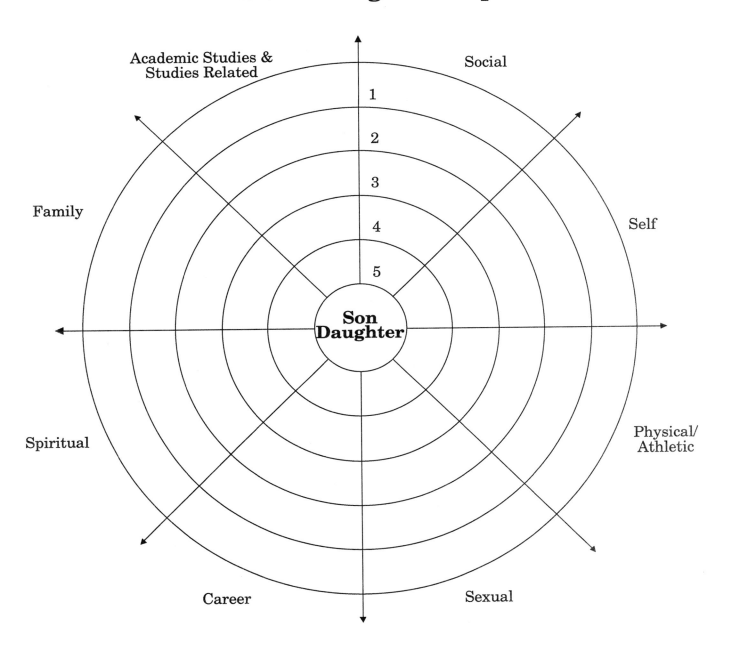

Academic Studies &
Studies Related

Social

1

2

3

4

5

Son
Daughter

Family

Self

Spiritual

Physical/
Athletic

Career

Sexual

DATE_____

LIFE-SPACE SITUATIONS QUESTIONNAIRE

Read the following statements and rate them with regard to how much subjective risk would be involved in this behavior for your daughter or son. Write the appropriate number from the scale below in front of each item.

When you have completed this exercise your EPB Worksheet will be similar to the example shown in Figure 5.

1   Would be no risk for him/her.
2   Would be a small risk for her/him.
3   I have no feelings one way or the other or I don't know
4   Would be some risk for him/her.
5   Would be a high risk for her/him.

EPB
Arena

Arena		#	Item
Acad	____	1.	Talking in class.
Acad	____	2.	Talking to a professor.
Soc	____	3.	Asking someone for a date.
Soc	____	4.	Confronting a roommate about a problem.
Soc	____	5.	Confronting a boy/girlfriend about a problem.
Soc	____	6.	Talking to strangers at a party.
Acad	____	7.	Taking tests.
Car	____	8.	Confronting a boss.
Self	____	9.	Making decisions.
Soc	____	10.	Giving compliments.
Self	____	11.	Trusting others.
Self	____	12.	Accepting compliments.
Self	____	13.	Asking for help.
Acad	____	14.	Writing a paper for class.
Acad	____	15.	Taking midterm or final exams.
Fam	____	16.	Confronting parents.
Self	____	17.	Saying "I love you".
Soc	____	18.	Confronting old friends.
Acad	____	19.	Registering for classes.
Spir	____	20.	Expressing your religious beliefs.
Car	____	21.	Choosing a career field.
Self	____	22.	Expressing your anger.
Phy	____	23.	Driving in a big city.
Self	____	24.	Expressing affection physically.
Phy	____	25.	Participating in a sport you're not very good at.
Phy	____	26.	Visiting the dentist.

EPB
Arena

Self	_____	27.	Admitting you were wrong.
Self	_____	28.	Showing your competence.
Self	_____	29.	Showing your weakness.
Soc	_____	30.	Returning a defective item to the store.
Self	_____	31.	Helping victims at an auto accident site.
Phy	_____	32.	Going skydiving.
Self	_____	33.	Receiving a parking ticket.
Car	_____	34.	Getting chewed out by your boss.
Soc	_____	35.	Breaking up a relationship.
Self	_____	36.	Making it on your own after graduation.
Fam	_____	37.	Behaving in ways your parents would disapprove of.
Self	_____	38.	Going for counseling.
Phy	_____	39.	Going caving.
Phy	_____	40.	Going rock climbing.
Self	_____	41.	Attending personal growth workshops.
Fam	_____	42.	Spending holidays with family.
Fam	_____	43.	Paying for college.
Phy	_____	44.	Beginning a fitness program.
Car	_____	45.	Applying for a job.
Sex	_____	46.	Having a sexual relationship.
Self	_____	47.	Experimenting with drugs.
Spir	_____	48.	Starting or stopping attending religious services.

Write any additional statements that would be rated 4 or 5 for your son or daughter.

Enter the risk level number (1-5) you selected for each item (1-48) on the EPB worksheet on the following page. For example, if you rated item #13, 'Asking for help', at the #4 risk level, you could put the #13 in EPB arena Self at level 4. (See sample sheet)

Transfer your responses to the Life-Space Situations Summary Sheet, page 185.

Figure 5

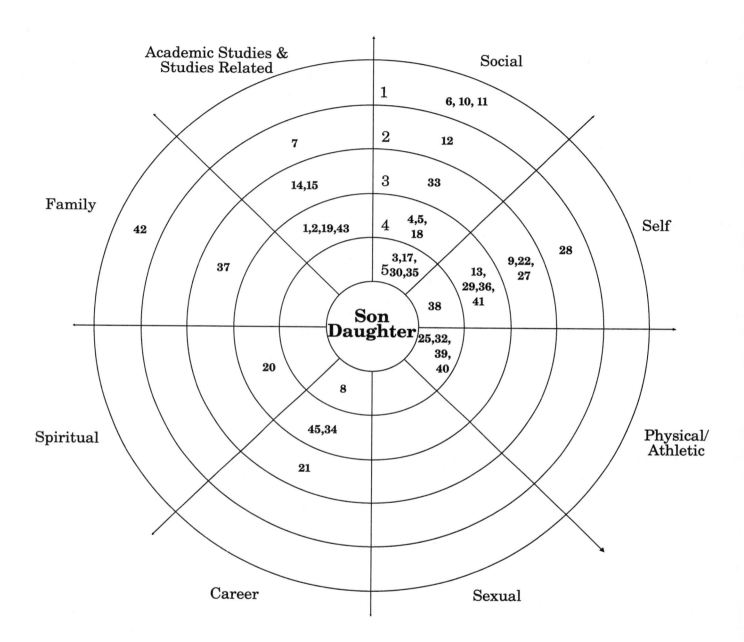

**EPB Worksheet - Example
Life-Space Situations**

EPB Worksheet
Life-Space Situations

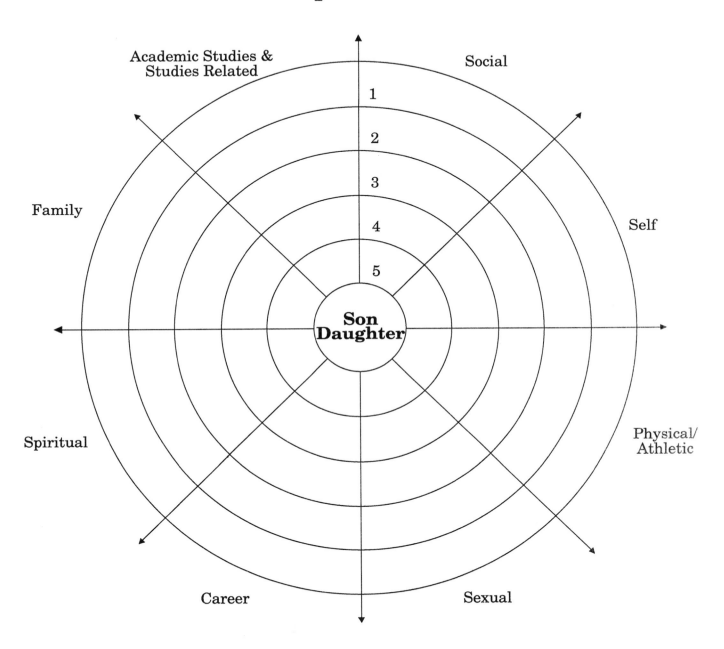

DATE _____

14

Look over your EPB worksheets for these two exercises. In which arenas do you find most of your son's or daughter's high (4 and 5) risk behaviors and in which do you find most of their low (1 and 2) risk behaviors? Are you finding out anything interesting about your child or about how much or how little you know about them? What might it be?

Focus on the behaviors you rated 1 or 2. Do you see these as strengths that can help them be a more successful person? Look these over until you can feel the strength of these behaviors as a part of your son or daughter.

Now focus on the behaviors that you rated 4 or 5. Picture your son or daughter doing these behaviors and feeling considerable fear and anxiety. As a parent you may be thinking, "I know I want to do what I can to help alleviate so much fear from my child. Yet I also know they must be the ones to deal with the fear; to make the changes necessary to go beyond fear. You can bet though that I want to support them in whatever ways are appropriate and contribute to my child's sense of competence and self-worth. " My guess is that is exactly what you want to do.

Now picture your son or daughter doing these behaviors and feeling anxiety only at the 1 or 2 level. Take a minute to experience how this reduction in fear and expansion of their competence and confidence doing this behavior would affect their life. How would knowing your child feels much more confident in him/herself and their ability to deal with situations affect your life? Select five behaviors where you feel a lowering of your child's fear and anxiety level will contribute significantly to their success in college and place them in the space below. After each behavior write down a specific action you will do to support your child in making this change.

I commit to working to expand my son's/daughter's boundaries for the following behaviors by:

Ex. Participating in class discussions - I will ask for my daughter's views on specific topics and truly listen to her views without having to voice my own or make mine right and her's wrong.

1.

2.

3.

4.

5.

Chapter 1 - EPB Mind Stretchers

1. Describe how you imagine your child felt when they first arrived on campus? How did you feel leaving your child and going home?
2. What is the main idea of this chapter?
3. How is your son or daughter going to the Academic Skills Center to improve their writing an example of expanding their perceptual boundaries?
4. Diagram the eight EPB life arenas.
5. How will your son or daughter create success for him/herself at Western? List their greatest strengths.
6. What criteria for each EPB arena would you use to assess your child's success their first semester in college? Be specific. Have you shared this with them?

SUCCESS TRIAD SUMMARY
Chapter 1 - The Great Transition

CHALLENGES:

1. Separate from parents, siblings, and other high school contacts that formed their support network.
2. Assume more adult responsibilities.
3. Make more decisions on their own.
4. Learn to function effectively in a new environment with different educational and social systems.
5. Establish a new support base of friends and acquaintances while maintaining appropriate ties with home.
6. Learn the new norms of their developing educational and social network.
7. Begin to answer the questions: Who am I? Where do I fit?

SUPPORT:

1. Help them to pack.
2. Transport their belongings to campus - especially items with personal significance even though you don't think they will need them.
3. Provision them with supplies needed for college; calculators, alarm clock, pens, pencils, typewriter, correcting tape or fluid, 3X5 note cards, reading/desk lamp, drapes, bedding, stapler, masking tape, thumb tacks, scotch tape, notebooks, letter writing paper, envelopes, stamps etc.
4. Computer - a special note on computers. In todays high tech world, a student without computer skills is at a significant deficit when doing course work as well as when the time comes to compete for jobs. If at all possible buy them a computer and the appropriate software for their discipline. A good word processing program is invaluable.

CARING:

1. Engage them in discussions of their hopes, fears, and expectations of college (due this before they leave for college if possible as well as after they have been away for awhile).
2. Clearly express your confidence in them and their ability to be successful in college.
3. Tell them you love them and will miss them. Let them also know how proud you are that they are going to college and beginning such an exciting time of life.

4.   Write them - cards and letters are very important to first term students. Send occasional gift packs of their favorites.

5.   Phone them - not too often but enough for them to know you care and for you to listen to how they are adjusting. Depending on your child and maybe your budget! calling once or twice a week the first term is common. If they are calling too often, listen carefully to them to see if there is a problem that might need attention. Start to limit the duration or frequency of calls but make sure you are not cutting them off from sharing real concerns with you.

18

NOTES

Chapter Two
Values

VALUES

If you were to look over the events of the past 24 hours, you would realize that you were in situations which required you to think, give your opinion, express how you felt, make decisions, and take action. Each of these thoughts, feelings, and behaviors were based on your attitudes, beliefs, and values.

Now try and put yourself into your son's or daughter's place. What do you imagine their last 24 hours were like? What decisions did they make? What values were challenged and maintained or which might be changing? As a student, they are facing and will continue to face many new situations. As they increase their understanding of their values, they will learn to deal more effectively with these experiences and to make the decisions that are productive and life-enhancing for them. Some values will be more important or clearer to them than others. Some they will act on more frequently.

The following exercises are intended to help you clarify and prioritize your values and those of your son or daughter.

PERSONAL VALUES

The following is a list of values, some of which you may feel more strongly about than others. Rate the degree to which these values are important in your personal life. Then rate the degree to which you perceive these values to be important in the personal life of your daughter or son.

1	Very important	3	Of little importance
2	Reasonably important	4	Not important at all

Parent/Son or Daughter

_____ Family	_____ Others' Opinions
_____ Friendship	_____ Excitement
_____ Happiness	_____ Comfortable Lifestyle
_____ Love Relationship	_____ Self-Control
_____ Self-Respect	_____ Courage
_____ Accomplishment	_____ Learning
_____ Moral Fulfillment	_____ World of Beauty
_____ Social Recognition	_____ Independence
_____ Honesty	_____ Security
_____ Inner Harmony	_____ Physical Fitness
_____ Freedom	_____ Health
_____ Equality	_____ Creativity
_____ World at Peace	_____ Variety
_____ Power	_____ Wealth
_____ Help Others	_____ Healthy Environment

CAREER VALUES

The following is a list of a wide variety of satisfactions that people obtain from their careers. Rate the degree of importance that you would assign to each career value for yourself using the scale below then do the same based on your perceptions of the importance of these career values for your daughter or son.

1 Very important in my choice of career
2 Reasonably important in my choice of career
3 Not very important in my choice of career
4 Not at all important in my choice of career

Parent/Son or Daughter

_____Work with others as a team   _____High pay

_____Public Contact   _____Excitement

_____Friendships with co-workers   _____Change and variety

_____Competition   _____Moral fulfillment

_____Make decisions   _____Time flexibility

_____Work under pressure   _____Help others

_____Power and authority   _____Travel

_____Influence people   _____Security

_____Learn new things   _____Status

_____Advancement   _____Creativity

_____Supervision   _____Work with things

_____Physical safety   _____Fast-pace work

_____Recognition   _____Location

_____Work with ideas   _____Parental leave benefits

_____Challenge

VALUES WORKSHEET

List five (5) personal values marked with a one (1).

Your Personal Values	Son's/Daughter's Values
1.	
2.	
3.	
4.	
5.	

List five (5) career values marked with a one (1).

Your Career Values	Son's/Daughter's Career Values
1.	
2.	
3.	
4.	
5.	

Enter the Personal and Career Values on the Summary Sheet, page 187.

Understanding your values can also be an effective way of learning about relationships. The next time you are in a conflict with someone, check to see if one of your values is being threatened. Another way is to think of this as your perceptual boundary in that arena is being pushed and you will decide whether you wish to expand, hold, or reduce that boundary. For example, if your daughter and her roommate are talking and the roommate is putting herself down repeatedly, your daughter may start feeling uncomfortable. As she checks herself out, she finds that she has a high value on self-respect and since her roommate is not showing herself the self-respect your daughter values, this value is threatened. Knowing which value is threatened also gives your daughter an opportunity to provide helpful, constructive feedback to her roommate. "Jane, I feel uncomfortable listening to you putting yourself down. I see many positive qualities in you and want you to stop being so hard on yourself."

Similarly, when you feel positive about your interactions, your values are often being supported and validated. For example, your son finds himself stimulated and alert during class. When checking his values, he becomes aware that three of his important values were met in the class; his value on learning, challenge, and respect. In this one class, the instructor challenged him intellectually, treated him and other classmates with respect and presented information in a way that made it interesting and easier to learn.

As you can see, all your feelings, thoughts, and behaviors can ultimately be related to how congruent they are with your values. For your son or daughter, college life presents them with many people, ideas, and situations, that will help them to clarify their values. It is a time in which they may try out new behaviors and values, some of which may be against those values you hold and want them to hold. As parents this can be a very challenging time. The above exercises can help you to see where major conflicts arise; where your values boundaries are tested by the experimentation of your child with his or her values boundaries. This is a time of experimentation for most students which can be pleasant or unpleasant as well as growth enhancing or growth restricting. The challenge for parents is to understand that experimenting with values is a normal developmental stage (see Chapter 6 Chickering) and that you cannot control what your child does while in college. Research indicates that most young people, after this period of experimentation, will adopt values of their own which are similar to those of their parents. To me this is encouraging if the values you imparted are decent and respectful of human growth and our responsibility to this planet. This may be a good time for you to honestly assess your values, how you are trying to encourage your children to have the same values, and whether or not you wish to change any of your values.

No matter what you personally decide to do about your own values, I hope you will listen carefully to your children. Encourage them to talk openly and honestly about their values and the struggles they may be having to determine what is right or wrong. I like to ask students to consider whether their values and the behaviors reflecting those values contribute to their health, happiness, and success. If not, I ask them to think about the value they hold that is so important they are willing to knowingly do things that are unhealthy for themselves. Often, once they get beyond curiosity it is their need for acceptance that is so valued. They are so afraid of not being accepted, liked, and fitting in that they will behave in ways that can jeopardize their growth and some times even their safety.

So listen to your children. Let me paraphrase what I have heard all too often from students. "I know I'm not sure of what I believe anymore. It can get so confusing. Do I do drugs, get involved sexually, change my major, drive with a drunk friend? Sometimes what I think is right for me doesn't fit or at least I don't think it does with my friends so I'm not willing to take the chance of being made fun of, being wrong, or losing my friends. I'd like to be able to talk to my parents. Not so much to have them tell me what to do but just to listen to me, to try to understand what I'm feeling. Instead and I think it is because they are scared for me, they tell me what I can do and can't do. Don't they understand I can do whatever I want? If I'm going to grow up to be a responsible, reasonably happy and successful adult, I must make these decisions on my own. But I don't want to make them in a vacuum. I need support from the people who know me best. I need encouragement to do what is best for me. And yes, I might even want to hear them say that they are afraid that what I'm doing might be harmful to me and that they won't support it because it jeopardized my safety. But you know, most of the things they get uptight about don't have a lot to do with safety. I wish they would really listen to me and try to understand. Parents just don't understand". **PARENTS JUST DON'T UNDERSTAND!** Work to listen until you do understand, remembering that understanding doesn't necessarily mean you agree.

Periodic review of values is helpful since values do change. During the first year of college, your son or daughter will be exposed to many people and situations that challenge their values and yours. This can be very uncomfortable at times. Yet, as you learn to listen more to your child you help them to learn about themselves and their values. They will become more competent at making decisions congruent with their values and that enhance their life. As a parent seeing and knowing you have been a positive influence in your child's growth and happiness is a fine reward.

GROUP PROCESS GUIDELINES
BALANCING SAFETY AND RISK

In order for your daughter and son to grow, there must be a constant attempt to balance risk and safety. Too little safety and they will not take the risks to grow; too much safety and they will feel constrained from taking the risks. Parents are responsible for establishing and insuring guidelines for physical and emotional safety. With these safety guidelines in place, your child can put their energy into the risks that have the potential for expanding boundaries in the arenas, and to the extent that they wish. The following paragraphs are from the *Expanding Perceptual Boundaries* text for students and shows how the principles of safety and risk manifest themselves in their classes.

"The Johari Window (Ingham and Luft) is a useful guide to individual and group safety as well as group process (Figure 6). Quadrant I, area of free activity, is appropriate and safe for you as an individual and the class as a group. Since the information in this quadrant is known to you and others it is public domain and non-threatening. The information contained in quadrant II is considered risky to others because they are taking the risk of giving you feedback about something of which you are not aware; bad breath for example. They risk your anger, shame, resentment, or rejection. However, this feedback can be very valuable to your growth. Remember that what you decide to do with the feedback is your responsibility. Quadrant III is risky for you because it involves sharing something private with your classmates. In class this will often be your opinion or supported view on a particular topic under discussion. Without you taking the risk to volunteer this information no one would know what you think. The information in the area of the unknown, quadrant IV, is not known to you or others. It resides in the unconscious and is not available for exploration in class.'

'For this class to be a productive learning experience, you and your classmates will need to go beyond the comfort and security of quadrant I. They will need to risk giving you feedback and you will need to risk volunteering your private thoughts and feelings. This is a reciprocal relationship which is as necessary for a good learning experience as it is for any healthy interpersonal relationship."

Your sons and daughters will take more of the risks necessary to grow if their home environment is supportive; not too safe because that says to the student "You aren't competent enough to do this thing so we will do it for you or protect you. We don't believe in you to be able to do this." As parents we must be careful not to limit or smother our children. On the other hand too little safety at home and the child can be overwhelmed. The message can come across as "We expect you to be able to do everything and do it perfectly." This sets up a situation in which the child feels compelled to take on all challenges and do all of them perfectly. Obviously this will lead to great stress since no one can accept all challenges presented and no one can do anything, much less everything, perfectly. Students whom I have worked with where this was the message they took from home, suffered extreme stress, had trouble relating to others since they were always competing to do better, often had suicidal thoughts, suffered low self-esteem, and held a great deal of anger toward their parents for putting such pressure on them. Parents were often not aware of these thoughts and feelings because the child would not want to disappoint the parents by 'being so imperfect.'

Some homes provide too little safety in another way. A significant minority of college students come from homes where physical, sexual, or emotional abuse was too often a part of their reality. For these students safety and security are of major importance and trusting others can be difficult. Parents of these students may be deluded to believe that their treatment of the child is correct and helpful, others don't even realize what they are doing is harsh and harmful, while others think the child "deserves" what they get. These parents generally have no idea of the deep emotional wounds they have inflicted on their children, the scars these children will carry the rest of their lives, and how this treatment interferes with their child's willingness and ability to develop into a healthy, competent, responsible adult.

Please check yourself and see if you are promoting growth, not fear and hostility by your verbal and physical interactions with your children. If you are not sure that your behaviors are healthy for your children or know for certain they aren't, you can make an appointment with a mental health professional or perhaps a member of the clergy trained to help you develop behaviors that will be healthier for you and your children. If you are interacting in ways that provide your son or daughter a sense of safety and security as well as a belief in themselves and their ability to meet new challenges, I hope you will appreciate the gift you have given to your child and yourself.

Figure 6

JOHARI WINDOW

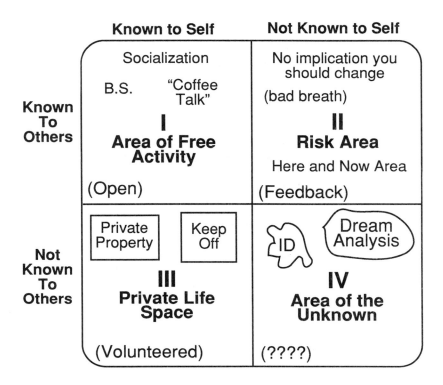

Chapter 2 - EPB Mind Stretchers

1. What are values?
2. From having talked with your son or daughter, relate a campus incident that clearly demonstrated they lived up to one of your values. Relate one where they behaved in a way that went against your values? How did you deal with each?
3. How are your daughter's or son's values related to decisions they make about careers, academic major, and even their friendships?
4. How does Quadrant II (Risk Area) compare with Quadrant III (Private Life Space) of the Johari Window?
5. How would you redesign your home environment to better balance safety and risk?
6. What do you think about your living up to your top personal and career values? What have you decided to do to be more congruent with your values? How will you share what you have learned with your child?

SUCCESS TRIAD SUMMARY
Chapter 2 - Values

CHALLENGES:

1. Examine their values in the presence of the often conflicting values of others.
2. Experiment with new behaviors that reflect different values as part of deciding what values are truly "their own".
3. Begin to prioritize their most important values as a clear expression of their emerging identity and career direction.
4. Understand how their values influence their choice of friends, classes, careers, majors, out of class activities etc.
5. Learn to manage their time effectively.

SUPPORT:

1. Provide the financial or material support to enable your daughter or son to participate in activities that reflect healthy values experimentation or deepening commitment.

CARING:

1. Frequently talk with your son or daughter about their values.
2. Listen to their struggles to define themselves thru their behaviors and values often in the face of conflicting values and behaviors from friends. Due this without dictating to them what is "right" and "wrong" and what they "can" or "cannot" do.
3. Help them to see how their values relate to their interests in academic majors, careers, friends, activities, and their personal decisions.
4. Encourage them to choose and support them verbally when they do choose values and behaviors that support healthy growth.

Time Management - Study Schedule

Complete by filling in fixed time as well as discretionary time items. Example of fixed time- classes, labs, team practice. Example of discretionary time- movies, dates, physical exercise, study time.

Time	Monday	Tuesday	Wednesday	Thursday	Friday	Saturday	Sunday
8:00							
9:00							
10:00							
11:00							
12:00							
1:00							
2:00							
3:00							

Time Management - Study Schedule

Complete by filling in fixed time as well as discretionary time items. Example of fixed time- classes, labs, team practice. Example of discretionary time- movies, dates, physical exercise, study time.

Time	Monday	Tuesday	Wednesday	Thursday	Friday	Saturday	Sunday
4:00							
5:00							
6:00							
7:00							
8:00							
9:00							
10:00							
11:00							

Chapter Three
Self-Assessment and Communication

SELF-ASSESSMENT AND COMMUNICATION

Chapter II, Values, began the process of assessing your familiarity with the values of your son or daughter and how similar their values are to yours. The exercises in this chapter, *Self-Assessment and Communication*, are intended to further your understanding of who your child is and why and how you relate the way you do. Because communication is how we let others know who we are and what we think and feel about ourselves, it has been addressed in this chapter.

SPENDING THEIR TIME

The activities your daughter or son enjoy and the way they spend their time tells you something about the values they have and the things that are important to them. Identifying their interests and values is an important "first step" toward making a satisfying career or personal lifestyle choice.

In the exercise that follows (see next page), list 15 activities that you think your child enjoys doing. Then, using the coding below, place a check in the appropriate column to the left of the activity. Any activity may receive more than one check.

Coding:

"A" Column:	The activity is done alone.
"SP" Column:	The activity is done with a special person.
"$" Column:	By your definition, the activity is expensive
"P" Column:	You approve of the activity.
"R" Column:	They took part in the activity within the last two weeks.

Once the exercise has been completed, total the number of "A's", "SP"'s and so on. The totals will serve as the basis for the items that you will list below the 15 activities.

SPENDING THEIR TIME

List 15 activities which you think your son or daughter would enjoy.

A	SP	$	P	R	
					1)
					2)
					3)
					4)
					5)
					6)
					7)
					8)
					9)
					10)
					11)
					12)
					13)
					14)
					15)
					Totals

Think about what you have learned about your daughter or son from doing this exercise. In the boxes below, write in any of the values or skills (everything you do requires certain skills) which you have listed in the activities column.

VALUES

1.

2.

3.

4.

5.

SKILLS

1.

2.

3.

4.

5.

Enter the values and skills on the Summary Sheet, page 187

FRAMEWORK OF PERSONALITY STRENGTHS

Your child has special strengths that make them different from other people. Very often these are not given adequate consideration when making decisions that involve the whole person (i.e., career, marriage, parenthood, lifestyle, etc.). Each strength says something about what kind of a person they are.

Read the following and check the individual strength in each area that describes them. Rate the degree of importance that you think they would assign to each using the scale below:

1 Very important
2 Reasonably important
3 Of little importance
4 Not important at all

1. **SPECIAL APTITUDES OR RESOURCES:**
   _____Having hunches or making guesses which usually turn out right
   _____Following through on these hunches
   _____Having a "green thumb"
   _____Sale ability
   _____Ability in mathematics
   _____Skill with hands in constructing or repairing things
   _____Other_____

2. **INTELLECTUAL STRENGTHS:**
   _____Applying reasoning ability to problem solving
   _____Intellectual curiosity
   _____Thinking about ideas and expressing them aloud or in writing
   _____Being able to accept new ideas
   _____Doing original or creative thinking
   _____Having the ability to learn and enjoy learning
   _____Accurate use of grammar - verbally or written
   _____Other_____

3. **EDUCATION, TRAINING, RELATED AREAS:**
   _____On-the-job training
   _____Special courses you have taken
   _____Self-education through study and organized reading
   _____Any high grades
   _____Any scholastic and related honors
   _____Other_____

4. **WORK, VOCATION, JOB OR POSITION:**
   _____Held part-time or full-time job
   _____Felt job satisfaction

_____Enjoying your work
_____Good relations with co-workers
_____Feelings of loyalty toward employer or organization
_____Pride in work and duties
_____Other_____

5. **AESTHETIC STRENGTHS:**
    _____Recognizing and enjoying beauty in nature, the arts or
          people
    _____Using aesthetic sense to enhance your home (room) and
          physical environment
    _____Other_____

6. **ORGANIZATIONAL STRENGTHS:**
    _____Developing and planning sensible short-range and long-
          range goals
    _____Carrying out orders, as well as giving them
    _____Experience in organizing enterprises, projects, clubs- social,
          political, or other
    _____Having held leadership positions in such organizations
    _____Other_____

7. **HOBBIES AND CRAFTS:**
    _____Any hobbies, crafts and related interests including any
          instruction or training in such crafts as weaving, pottery,
          and jewelry making
    _____Other_____

8. **EXPRESSIVE ARTS:**
    _____Any type of dancing
    _____Any form of writing (stories, essays, poetry)
    _____Sketching, painting, sculpture, modeling with clay
    _____Ability to improvise music or play a musical instrument,
          definite rhythmic ability
    _____Other_____

9. **HEALTH:**
    _____Good health
    _____Seeking adequate medical treatment at once when needed
    _____Yearly medical check-ups
    _____Good eating habits
    _____Other_____

10. **SPORTS AND OUTDOOR ACTIVITIES:**
    _____Active participation in outdoor activities and sports,
          camping and hunting
    _____Regular exercise program

_____Active participation in organized sports
_____Awareness of sports and sports players
_____Other_____

11.   **IMAGINATIVE AND CREATIVE STRENGTHS:**
_____Using creativity and imagination for new and different ideas
      in relation to home, family, job, or vacation
_____Working on developing and extending your imagination and
      creative abilities
_____Other_____

12.   **RELATIONSHIP STRENGTHS:**
_____Encourage people
_____Ability to meet people easily
_____Ability to make people feel comfortable
_____Ability to talk freely with strangers
_____Good relations with neighbors
_____Treating people with consideration, politeness, and respect
      at all times
_____Being aware of the needs and feelings of others
_____Being able to really listen to what others have to say
_____Helping others to be aware of their strengths and
      abilities as well as their shortcomings or problems
_____Relating to people as individuals, regardless of sex, creed, or
      race
_____Giving people the feeling that you understand them
_____A willingness to express your feelings with others
_____Being honest with people
_____Other_____

13.   **EMOTIONAL STRENGTHS:**
_____Ability to give as well as to receive affection or love
_____Being able to feel and express a wide range of emotions
_____Being able to do or express things on the spur of the
      moment
_____Ability to put yourself in the other person's shoes, to feel
      what they feel
_____Understanding the role of your feelings and emotions in
      everyday life
_____Other_____

14.   **OTHER STRENGTHS:**

_____Sense of humor
_____Able to laugh at yourself and to take kidding at your own
      expense
_____Liking to adventure or pioneer, to explore new horizons or
      to try new ways of doing things
_____Perseverance or stick-to-itiveness, having a strong drive to

get things done

_____Ability to manage finances, evidenced by investments and
savings, among other things

_____Knowledge of languages or of different people and cultures,
through travel, study, or reading

_____Ability to speak in public or make a public presentation

_____Making the best of your appearance by means of grooming
and good choices of clothes

_____Other_____

Of your daughter's or son's strengths, which three do you admire most?

1.

2.

3.

What three strengths do you think he or she wants people to recognize and
appreciate most?

1.

2.

3.

Of all the strengths listed, which three would you most like to see them
improve?

1.

2.

3.

List the three personality strengths you consider their strongest asset in
helping them be successful in a career.

1.

2.

3.

List the three personality strengths you consider their strongest asset in helping them be successful in dealing with other people.

1.

2.

3.

(Enter on Summary Sheet, page 187).

COMMUNICATION

Communication is an essential part of human interaction. In fact, all of your interactions are a way of communicating. Even though approximately 70+ percent of your communication is non-verbal, the 30-percent which is verbal is accorded more importance in the educational system and in society in general. Hopefully you will begin to appreciate and act on the wealth of non-verbal communication in your environment.

For now, let's take a closer look at your verbal communication. Since your first English class, you were taught to write in the third person and penalized for writing in the first person (unless, of course, it was for the obligatory *"How I Spent My Summer"* essay). Over the years, you have paid a price for learning this type of written communication, which you so successfully generalized to your speech. You lost a sense of responsibility for your innermost thoughts, feelings, behaviors when you said "you" when you really meant "I". Only through the use of appropriate "I" statements can you take ownership and responsibility for your thoughts, feelings, and behaviors and make contact, true contact, with another person. This is the kind of contact Martin Buber called "I to Thou".

Let's briefly examine the use of "it", "they", "we", "you", and "I" statements. What does an "it" statement do? It impersonalizes and objectifies something. There is no human warmth or dimension to "it". Yet, you actually talk about your own body using "it". "It hurts", referring to a pain in your leg.

"They" statements separate us from other human beings. It may be to give credit or blame. "They never do anything right". "They're always the ones who succeed". But it says "they" are in some significant way different than I am or we are. We can also use "they" statements to rely on some other group as an authority figure for their credibility. "They have shown that research says...."

"We" statements are the first ones that you use where there is an inclusion or getting closer to others. Be careful with "we" statements that they are being used appropriately. Are you making a "we" statement and truly knowing that other people want to be included in it? "We support the President's actions" If you were talking for your friends at work on what grounds are you stating that? Or are you stating it just to have a stronger position, and not really being concerned at all with what the other people at work think? You may notice couples in relationships misusing "we". One person says "we want to go out to dinner tonight," without even having talked to the other person in the relationship. "We" can be misused and used as a way of manipulating people. "We" can also help draw us together and show unity.

"You" statements you would think, indicate that you are talking to someone else. If I'm talking to you and I say, "Is this what you like?" and you respond, "Yes," it is very clear that I was talking to you. You may notice that one of *your* most common ways of referring to *yourself* though, is by using the pronoun "you". "You get upset with the negativism at work but what can you do", when talking to your friend. In this example the "you" is clearly *you* and would be much clearer if worded "I get upset...". "You" is also a blaming word as well as a giving-credit word. Many arguments in relationships get heated and defensive because the interaction begins with "You did something I don't like." "You didn't do what I wanted you to." Instead of making a statement about how you are feeling at the moment, about what you're thinking, you use "you" to blame and put responsibility on someone else.

"I" statements are the only way in which you can really take ownership for what you are thinking, what you are feeling, and what you are doing. All the others have with them the ability to avoid ownership or responsibility for what you are saying. If I say that, "We believe that the politics of the President are way out of line," and I perceive you as not liking what I just said, I can always say, "Well, I'm not really talking about me, I'm talking about people in general or other people, 'they'." You may notice that as you start using more "I" statements, that you will feel much more responsibility for your thoughts, your actions and your beliefs. This is one way of getting in touch with and regaining your own personal power. Therefore, it is an important part of the expanding perceptual boundaries process of empowering you to be successful personally as well as in communication with your daughter or son. By reviewing this chapter with your child and supporting each other in the use of "I" statements, you will be helping your daughter or son to develop a greater sense of ownership and responsibility for her/his behavior which will empower them and assist them in being successful in college.

For this next week, be aware of your interpersonal communications, especially "I" statements. Whenever you are referring to something that you believe, that you feel or that you experience, use "I" statements, not "you," not "it," not "we". This will be difficult to do, but if approached with commitment and effort you will make significant progress during the week. One of the main reasons that this is so difficult is that this is a very personal risk, it's a high level risk putting yourself on the line for your statements, your beliefs, your actions. Understand, too, that each of us grew up in a system, an educational as well as societal one, that encourages us not to take responsibility in our communication for our actions. When you're taught to write in the second or third person all the way through school and anytime you start talking about "I", you're considered to be bragging or self-centered, you get the mistaken notion that being in touch with your own feelings or thoughts is somehow out-of-line and that the only way to do it appropriately, is to use disowning words. So for the next week, concentrate heavily on communication and be aware of the communication of other people and you'll notice how they use "you" statements, "we" statements, and "they" statements, for different purposes.

READ THIS SECTION OVER AGAIN AND AGAIN UNTIL YOU ARE USING APPROPRIATE "I" STATEMENTS. OF ALL THE MATERIAL IN THIS BOOK, THIS USE OF "I" STATEMENTS CAN BE THE MOST IMPORTANT IN COMMUNICATING WITH YOUR SON OR DAUGHTER IN AN ASSERTIVE AND CARING MANNER AND CONTRIBUTE GREATLY TO THE DEVELOPMENT OF A CLOSER, HEALTHIER RELATIONSHIP WITH YOUR CHILD. SUCH A RELATIONSHIP WILL CONTRIBUTE SIGNIFICANTLY TO YOUR CHILD'S SUCCESS IN COLLEGE AND LIFE.

Chapter 3 - EPB Mind Stretchers

1. What were three values you identified from your child's activities list?
2. In your own words, what is the importance of communicating with ownership?
3. How is the use of "I" statements related to the Johari Window, Quadrant III (Private Life Space)? Now apply this to communicating to your son or daughter.
4. What are the individual characteristics of usage of the five pronouns used in this chapter?
5. Would you predict it will be difficult or easy, comfortable or uncomfortable for you to use "I" statements? Will it be easier with your spouse, children, friends, co-workers, strangers? Why?
6. Do you agree with this chapter's emphasis on using ownership words? What from this chapter is most helpful to you? Are you making this statement after giving the suggestions a fair try?

SUCCESS TRIAD SUMMARY
Chapter 3 - Self-Assessment and Communication

CHALLENGES:

1. Develop new and enhance existing skills.
2. Begin to understand the connection between skills and academic and career decisions.
3. Communicate using "I" statements when talking about their own feelings and thoughts.
4. Take responsibility for their behavior and reflect this in their communications.
5. Empower themselves and enhance their self-esteem by communicating using clear and positive statements.
6. Replace negative self-talk and criticism of others with positive validations of self and others.

SUPPORT:

1. Provide the finances or equipment necessary to help your son or daughter enhance their skills and sense of self-esteem (ex. buy a new clarinet for your son's music major and participation in the college orchestra; fund your daughter's participation in a weekend retreat on eliminating self-defeating behaviors).

CARING:

1. Use "I" statements when communicating with your daughter or son.
2. Listen openly and without prejudice to your child.
3. Respond openly and honestly and with "I" statements.
4. Validate their skills and competencies and personality strengths to encourage them to believe in themselves and keep growing.
5. Clearly communicate your love and support.

46

NOTES

Chapter Four
Loneliness

LONELINESS, THE "NAMELESS FEAR" HITS 30 PERCENT OF WMU STUDENTS

Loneliness, to one extent or another, is common to all of us. Sometimes thinly veiled behind our anxieties, at other times embedded in our deepest fears, loneliness impacts our lives in many ways. Sociologists and psychologists agree that loneliness is widespread in our society. At Western Michigan University, as well as at other major universities, loneliness has reached epidemic proportions with consequences affecting students' self-esteem, interpersonal relationships, motivation, productivity, and happiness.

It seems reasonable to assume that something as pervasive as loneliness would have been researched extensively and sound remedies found to effectively deal with eliminating it. This is not the case.

As part of a larger, ongoing Student Needs Assessment conducted at WMU over seven years, valuable information regarding student loneliness on campus was obtained. Thirty percent of students responding reported feeling lonely half or more of the time - a percentage indicative of an epidemic. But what is loneliness? Can it be cured? Let's take a closer look at loneliness, its nature, symptoms, and possible solutions.

Definition and Characteristics

Loneliness has been defined as the "feeling of being alone and disconnected or alienated from positive persons, places, or things." (Weiss, 1973) Loneliness is a response to relational deficit and is not to be confused with being alone by choice. Different forms of loneliness are responsive to different remedies. The absence of a close emotional attachment, characterized as the "loneliness of emotional isolation," can only be remedied by the integration of another emotional attachment. Conversely, the form of loneliness associated with the absence of an engaging social network, "the loneliness of social isolation" can be remedied by access to such a network.

The symptoms of the loneliness of emotional and social isolation differ. Emotional isolation is characterized by a feeling of distress and a fear of abandonment. It is a pervasive apprehensiveness, a "nameless fear," that may also force the individual into some sort of physical activity as a channel for his/her jumpiness. A vigilance to threat is common and the individual may be unable to relax enough to sleep. The student may report feeling empty, hollow or dead inside. Emotional outbursts of sadness, or frustration and anger may show up as crying spells or hostile acts. Self-confidence is down while defensiveness and insecurity are up. Mood swings are common. Eating and sleeping patterns may be disrupted and the individual may experience a need to talk to someone about personal matters.

Social isolation is characterized by feelings of boredom, exclusion, aimlessness and marginality. In social isolation, daily tasks, whether to clean house, balance the checkbook or study, become boring without the affirmation of others. The student is often unhappy, restless, anxious and may find it difficult to make decisions. Friendships become more important, yet the individual may be frustrated with his/her success at making friends.

Who Are The Lonely?

Are the above characteristics descriptive of the behavior you are observing or hear about from your son or daughter? Perhaps he/she is one of the lonely. If so, they are not alone. Woodward and others in their research on loneliness have identified college students as the loneliest group in our society. The results of the WMU Student Needs Assessment of 1981, 1984, and 1987, certainly support this finding. In terms of loneliness theory, it is logical and consistent that college students would be the loneliest group. This is the first time many of them have been away from home for a prolonged length of time. And this time their leaving symbolizes a permanent change in their relationship with you, their parents, as well as with their siblings and hometown friends. All the important support groups and individual ties in their life are severed or strained. Their base of security and interpersonal support are gone - they are confronted by many uncertainties about life and the expectations for them in the new environment at WMU. Decisions about careers, academic majors, values, finances and relationships seem pressing and demanding of resolution. They are in a developmental period of insecurity, uncertainty, life re-evaluation, and loss of self-confidence. Though also an exciting, challenging and growth producing time, their potential for experiencing the loneliness of emotional and/or social isolation is great. (Figure 7)

According to Maslow's Hierarchy of Needs (Figure 8), people will satisfy their physiological needs first, then their needs for safety, social acceptance, esteem, and self-actualization in that order. Loneliness has a major impact on social acceptance and esteem needs. Since success in academics is generally a self-actualization need, you may notice your daughter or son reporting having difficulty concentrating on their studies until their social acceptance and esteem needs are more satisfactorily met.

This isn't to say they won't be able to do their coursework successfully if still lonely, but it does imply that their potential for being successful academically and using their energies efficiently may be enhanced by meeting their social acceptance and esteem needs.

Retention and Loneliness

Alexander Astin and the American College Testing Service have conducted extensive research on attrition and retention over many years. Their findings have been consistent. The four major causes for students leaving school are isolation (loneliness and depression), dissonance, academic boredom, and irrelevancy. Students tend to persist in college if they are making progress toward an educational and career goal, achieve academic success, know program options, use academic advising services, feel a sense of belonging and personal worth, and have a positive identity with high self-esteem. The most significant reason cited by students for staying was having contact with a *caring faculty member.*

If your child does not feel like she/he belongs, feels lonely and is bored, he/she is less likely to stay at WMU. It also seems possible that academic performance, motivation, and classroom attentiveness would improve if students were less lonely and devoted more energy to these endeavors.

Minimizing Loneliness

Individual loneliness cannot be avoided, but its duration, intensity and scope can be minimized. You can be of assistance to your child by being aware of the different kinds of loneliness and sharing with them the following list of suggestions for college students:

1. *Admit it..* Being aware you are lonely, and understanding loneliness can be a first and effective step in dealing with it. In fact many first year students are relieved that they are not alone, that other students are experiencing one or more kinds of loneliness.
2. *Take chances..* Risks at establishing relationships are necessary. Accept rejection and bounce back. Make your feelings and needs known.
3. *Depend on yourself..* Give things a try. If you need help, ask but be sure you have made a good effort at accomplishing the task. As your sense of competence and self-responsibility increases your self-confidence will grow.
4. *Lower your unrealistic expectations.* Avoid the perfection trap - especially in interpersonal relationships.
5. *Find outside interests.* Get involved and participate actively.
6. *Identify with a community.* This may be friends, family, work or a religious group. Their strength, stability and support can be helpful.
7. *Be with people who care about you.* Though often overlooked in the rush to complete concrete tasks such as homework or studying for tests, research supports the positive impact caring people can have on retention and performance.
8. *Communicate with people.* This is the best way to know others and to be known, which is how to make friends and minimize loneliness. Call or write family and friends. This behavior decreases each year in college until they beg to hear from you!

IMPORTANT NOTE TO PARENTS: MAIL AND PHONE CALLS ARE VERY IMPORTANT TO FIRST TERM STUDENTS! Your child needs to know someone and preferably a number of people back home still remember and care about her/him. Letters, notes, cards, phone calls and food or gift packages from home mean so much. Though these communications also will be appreciated in later years, they are very helpful in easing the loneliness and stress of the transition from high school to college.

9. *Be positive about yourself and others.* You do want friends, don't you? Being around someone who is consistently negative can be a strain on friendships. Cultivate a more positive attitude.

10. *Find someone you can talk with about personal concerns.* It is not healthy physically or emotionally to bottle-up feelings. Talk with a good friend, family member, clergy, or a counselor in the Counseling Center.

11. *Visit home occasionally.* Avoid going home every weekend because you need this time to establish new friendships and activities.

For more specific information on loneliness, Figure 9, lists the characteristics and possible helpful interventions for seven kinds of loneliness.

In addition, professional counseling may be very beneficial where loneliness interferes with your daughter's or son's ability to be happy and productive, especially in cases of deep emotional loneliness.

Support Groups

Faculty, staff, student leaders and others who work with students can comprise important support groups or individuals. Such support, whether provided by a club, team, campus organization, friends, or faculty or staff members, can help your son or daughter to feel a sense of belonging. It also can aid in dealing with difficulties and assist in exploring, understanding and acting upon social, emotional and cognitive dimensions of various developmental tasks. Support groups provide the opportunity for the social contact necessary to minimize the loneliness of social isolation. Often, from these contacts, deep friendships develop which will help your child deal with emotional isolation.

One mistake often made by first year students is to devote themselves exclusively to academics to the neglect or elimination of other endeavors. Research over many years supports students being more well-rounded. Students who work part-time (10-15 hrs wk), belong to a club, fraternity, sorority, team or are actively involved in the out-of-class life of their university tend to have higher grade point averages and retention rates than students who strictly do academics. I think by now you can see that your child cannot adjust well to college without being involved in activities that give them a sense of belonging, competence, personal self-worth, and satisfaction.

Social System

In addition to the effects individuals, faculty, staff, student leaders and others can have on reducing your child's loneliness, changes in the social system or social milieu may be helpful. For example, Drop/ Add has been a student complaint for years. On the recommendation of a committee, changes were made in the Drop/Add procedure which resulted in a smoother and less irritating experience. Changes might be needed in the University's policies, procedures and environment (physical and emotional) so your child feels like a cared-about, significant, responsible and respected participant in the educational mission of their university.

If there are things at college you would like to see changed, call or write the appropriate office being as specific as possible about what is bothering you or your child and what you want done. If you are unsure about who is responsible, call the Vice President for Student Services office as this person is responsible for student related issues and can refer you to the appropriate office for your specific concern. Also be aware that calling or writing about things you or your child have been pleased with is appreciated and helps insure continuation of good efforts.

Summary

Loneliness is a widespread phenomena in our society and your sons or daughters, as college students, are members of the loneliest group. In order for them to meet their academic, personal and career needs more fully, it is important that they feel like they belong at Western, have definite career and academic plans, perceive a respect, caring and concern for them from faculty and staff, and are involved in the academic and social life of their university.

Chapter 4 - EPB Mind Stretchers

1. What is the definition of loneliness?
2. Explain why college students are the loneliest group in our society?
3. How is loneliness related to academic success?
4. Diagram the support groups, as in Figure 7, your child had in high school and the ones they have established at Western? Are there unmet needs you are aware of? How can you be supportive?
5. What other ideas do you have to help your son or daughter deal effectively with loneliness?
6. What two ideas in this chapter were most helpful to you?

SUCCESS TRIAD SUMMARY
Chapter 4 - Loneliness

CHALLENGES:

1. Be aware of the kind(s) of loneliness they are experiencing, understand that this is normal, and do what is necessary to minimize the negative feelings associated with loneliness.
2. Take risks which promise to help them grow as a person so they can cope more effectively with loneliness in the future.
3. Be open and honest in their communications.
4. Develop some intimate relationships with friends and get involved in extra-curricular activities.

SUPPORT:

1. Provide the monies to pay for more phone calls the first term than you think your daughter or son will make the next term.
2. Provide funds for an occasional trip home.
3. Provide funds for you to visit during homecoming or parents' day.

CARING:

1. Listen carefully for signs of loneliness: not fitting in, has no friends, difficulty concentrating on studies, anxious or fearful with no apparent reason, talks mostly of missing high school friends or you, plans to come home frequently etc.
2. Validate their feelings without having to solve their problem for them.
3. Review things they can do to minimize loneliness and encourage them to choose one or two to act on - then check back with them in a week to see how they are progressing.
4. Let them know you love them and miss them also.
5. Encourage their healthy involvement in extra-curricular activities, a part-time job etc. which will increase their contact with others.
6. Let them know they are welcome home while encouraging them to stay on campus to develop new friendships (do this gradually if at first they seem to have no friends at college or are very resistant).
7. Encourage them to talk with a counselor if they seem depressed and unhappy for more than two weeks.

WMU Student Transition from High School to WMU in Terms of Support Groups

Figure 7

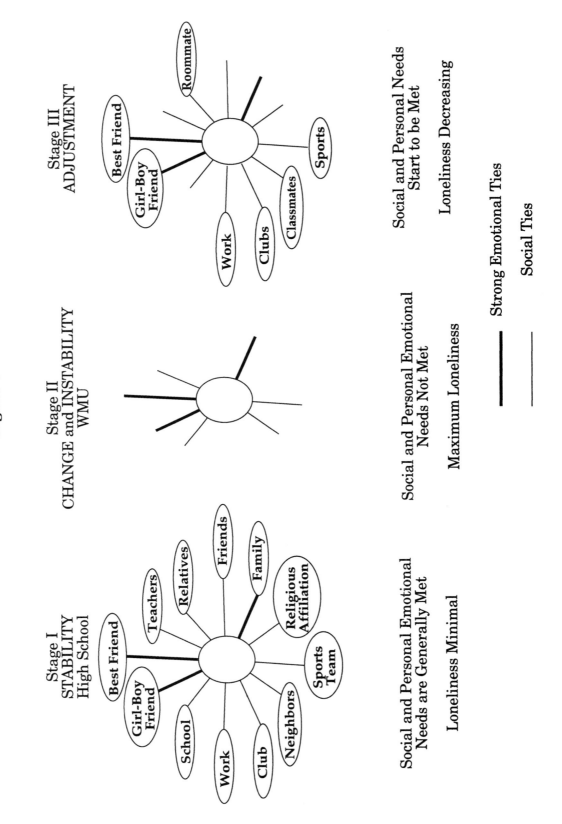

Stage I
STABILITY
High School

Stage II
CHANGE and INSTABILITY
WMU

Stage III
ADJUSTMENT

Social and Personal Emotional
Needs are Generally Met

Loneliness Minimal

Social and Personal Emotional
Needs Not Met

Maximum Loneliness

Social and Personal Needs
Start to be Met

Loneliness Decreasing

Strong Emotional Ties

Social Ties

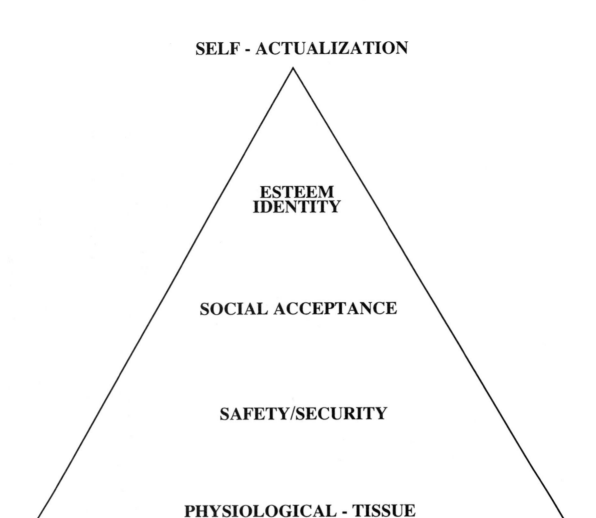

SELF - ACTUALIZATION

ESTEEM
IDENTITY

SOCIAL ACCEPTANCE

SAFETY/SECURITY

PHYSIOLOGICAL - TISSUE

HIERARCHY OF NEEDS
Dr. Abraham H. Maslow

Figure 8

Loneliness and the College Student

Kind	Characteristics	Intervention
Characterological	Shy Marginality Non-Assertive Frightened Self-Alienated	Learn Self-Responsibility Assertiveness Training Longer Term Counseling Develop Self-Worth
Situational Loneliness	Symptoms of Social or Emotional Isolation	Loneliness Orientation Loss/Grief Orientation Counseling Join Groups Keep Busy Change Situation
Social Isolation	Boredom Exclusion Marginality Restlessness Uncertainty Difficulty Making Friends Imitative Isolated	Loneliness Orientation Admit Loneliness Develop Internal Locus of Control Join Clubs, Organizations Raise Social Expectations Stop Comparing Self to Others Develop Competence Open, Honest Communication Take Risks
Anomie	Confused Don't Know How to Behave Strong Likes and Dislikes Anxious Normlessness Orderless Society Meaninglessness of Life Relationships Now Unpredictable	Values Clarification Indentify Compatable Friends

Figure 9

Loneliness and the College Student

Kind	Characteristics	Intervention
Alienation	Angry Rejected Rejecting of Society and Culture Self-Righteous Isolation Powerlessness Distrustful Pessimistic	Family Counseling Counseling Inclusion in Activities Group Work
Emotional Isolation	Fear of Abandonment Pervasive Apprehensiveness Defensiveness Empty, Hollow Feeling Inside Concentration Difficulty Physical Activity to Drain off Anxiety Emotional Outbursts Insecure Less Self-Confident Mood Swings Eating and Sleeping Patterns Disrupted Pressure- Feel you could Explode Need to talk to Someone about Personal Concerns Substance Abuse	Loneliness Orientation Support Groups Assertiveness Training Communication Skills Enhanced Self-Concept Enhancement Competence Building Lower Expectations of Self Loss/Grief Orientation Counseling Relationship/Intimacy Work Take Risks
Existential Loneliness	Feel Alone Question the Meaning of Life Feel Separated from Nature and Other People	Competence Building Decrease Dependence Recognize Need for Interdependence Establish Identity Develop Vocational and Lifestyle Meaning

Figure 9 (con't)

Chapter Five
Stress Management

STRESS MANAGEMENT

Stress management has become a popular topic in recent years. Courses, workshops, and books will promise to help you reduce the stress in your life. Reducing stress when your life is too stressful is a very good and healthy idea. However, stress isn't always bad. To win the Michigan Lottery for $5,000,000 would create a jubilant response in most of us. This response has a physical part to it that is similar whether the news is good or bad. We would experience an increase in heart rate, pulse, blood pressure, adrenaline production, and perspiration. So whether you win the lottery or flunk your final exam, the stress on your body is similar.

Because many of us envision the good life of being in college; the parties, sports, opportunities to learn and grow, the beautiful campuses, the holiday breaks, long summer vacations, informal gatherings of friends, etc. we tend to forget how stressful college is, especially for first year students. Understanding the stress caused by the transition from high school to college, the disruption of all personal relationships, the demands to perform academically and socially and perhaps athletically, the adjustment to a new environment and new systems of communication, authority, power, and the social and intellectual developmental tasks of young adults will enable you as a parent to be more supportive of your daughter or son.

Your support in the area of stress is consistent with the goal of the book; the ability of your son or daughter to manage stress in order to optimize their potential for success. We will look at the environmental and learned sources of stress and the physical and behavioral consequences of too much stress or distress. After this, you will use the EPB worksheets to plot your assessment of your child's situational stress as measured by the modified Holmes-Rahe Social Readjustment Scale and their personal stress as measured by the Life-Space Situation Scale. (Chapter 1)

Physical sources of stress are in your child's environment and their own bodies. A tornado could be the source of much stress if they were in its path. Sometimes, however, physical stresses are more subtle. The noise created by cars, stereos, TV's, and the human voice also contribute to their stress level. If you have ever lived in a college residence hall, you will appreciate how noisy it can get, especially at night. Students have told me that it is very difficult to get to bed before 1 or 2 a.m. most nights. For students with early morning classes this creates a real stress on their bodies. Often they will have the ability to increase or decrease their physical stress level within minutes. There are times, though, as those of you living in apartments or with large families know, when the ability to control the level of stress producers is in someone else's control. This lack of control in itself is a source of stress for many of us, your sons and daughters included.

An illness or injury is a physical source of stress that most of us would say is out of our control. Who would decide to be ill? Yet, more and more evidence is being accumulated to indicate we may have more control over such seemingly uncontrollable events than previously believed. This seems to imply a close relationship between physical stress and our personal thoughts and actions, and health.

These personal thoughts and actions are learned; parents, teachers, friends, siblings, relatives, religious leaders, and the advertising media can be powerful shapers of our thinking. Much of what your child has learned about their world and themselves is helpful in managing the level of stress in their lives. If he or she learned to add, subtract, and multiply and to trust themselves and others, they can avoid much potential stress from everyday financial transactions. If they learned that people can't be trusted, and they can't do basic adding, subtracting, or multiplying, they will find their everyday financial transactions stressful and unpleasant. This is because some of their learning has been inadequate or misdirected in preparing them to deal effectively with their world.

Now you may be thinking that this is true for everyone so why bring it up here. You are right that we all learned some things about ourselves and our world that haven't been helpful and have created stress for us. So let me ask you why you haven't unlearned the stressful and learned new, healthier thoughts and actions? If our children are to do better at reaching their potential, living a less stressful, more productive and happier life, they will need assistance in learning healthier behaviors and attitudes.

As you discuss the exercises, "Your Personal Rights" and "Irrational Beliefs" with your spouse, friends or your child, note what you have learned that is helpful to you in order to support your child's leading a healthier and less stressful life and what is not helpful. And while you are at it, why not do something good for yourself. Are you willing to change some stress producing thoughts, attitudes, and actions for more life-enhancing thoughts, attitudes, and actions? Yes. Good.

The physical and behavioral consequences of distress - too much stress - can be very harmful. Strokes, heart attacks, high blood pressure, and even some forms of cancer are stress related. We know from research at Western that in October significantly more students go to the Health Center and the Counseling Center than any other month. It is believed that one reason for this is young people who are basically healthy take about six to eight weeks to get run down from the stress of college. So as a parent be aware your son or daughter will most likely have their first college cold in October. Of course you can encourage them to get plenty of rest and eat well but as a first year college student would you have taken that advice from your parents when so much was going on you didn't want to miss anything! Behaviorally, irritation, defensiveness, withdrawal, even violence can be stress relate. There are many different ways to manage stress in your life. It is important to understand what actions to choose and when it is appropriate to choose them.

There are four major strategies for coping with stress that you will use and have used at various times: (1) non-productive escapes, (2) changing the stressful situation, (3) removing yourself from the stressful situation, and (4) changing your response to the stressful situation. Our focus will be on how to reduce stress by changing responses to the stressful situation. But an understanding of the other three strategies can be useful.

(1) The strategy of using non-productive escapes such as alcohol and other drugs, denial, and violence can provide some temporary sense of relief but doesn't solve any problems and can actually create more problems. As you complete the exercises in this chapter, you will realize that first year students are under considerable stress. The fact that alcohol and other drugs give temporary relief from stress makes them very seductive. The more adequately your son or daughter manage the stress in their lives, the less likely they are to abuse substances. Substance abuse is a serious problem and more complicated than can be presented here, but for most students stress reduction would contribute to less abuse of substances.

(2) Instead of avoiding dealing directly with their stress as in the non-productive strategies, they may be able to change the stressful situation. If your spouse is continually complaining that you leave your clothes all over the room, you can decide to put them away. If your child's roommate is complaining about clothes being taken without permission, your son or daughter can ask permission if they wish to borrow some clothes. The stress of being complained at is quickly eliminated.

(3) A useful, though often inconvenient and emotionally painful, strategy is to remove themselves from the stressful situation. If you are sitting in a very uncomfortable seat, you can change seats. If your child's relationship no longer provides the satisfaction it once did, and is now very stressful, they can terminate the relationship.

(4) The fourth strategy involves changing their response to the stressful situation. There are many techniques which can be employed; some provide a temporary reduction in stress, others provide a more long-term reduction because actual attitudes and beliefs change. Muscle relaxation, imagery, use of relaxation tapes, and deep breathing can provide quick stress reduction in many situations and are very useful to reduce, for example, test anxiety.

As your child acts more assertively and eliminates certain irrational beliefs, she/he will reduce some of the stress in their life. For example, she may feel stress around a certain "friend" who frequently belittles her, but she doesn't say anything because she is afraid of being rejected and not finding another "friend". She can reduce much of this stress by eliminating the irrational belief of not being able to find another friend, by realizing she certainly can make other friends, and by directly asking this person to stop belittling her.

Page 69 lists ten of the most popular irrational ideas or beliefs people hold. Which ones do you think your child believes? How do they create stress by believing and acting on them? The following page lists personal rights. Do they believe they have these rights and do they then act on them? Stress can be created when they do not assert their rights.

Above are some of the techniques your daughter or son can use to change their responses to a stressful situation. Keep in mind that some strategies and techniques will be easier to implement than others. Yet, if they wish to reduce the stress in their lives so that they live a happier, more productive, and perhaps longer life, they will have to make a commitment to change. Are you willing to assist them? If so, write three changes you commit to making for yourself and then ask them to write three for themselves:

Example: I commit to doing twenty minutes of visualization each day.

I commit to talking to my supervisor about my desire for more specific feedback about my job performance.

I commit to being kinder to myself and not putting so much pressure on myself to be perfect.

LIST HERE:

1.

2.

3.

SOCIAL READJUSTMENT RATING SCALE*

Circle the EPB Scale number and the Stress Points number for any of the events that have taken place in the life of your son or daughter in the past year.

EPB ARENA	EPB Scale		Stress Points
Fam	5	1. Death of spouse	100
Fam	4	2. Divorce	73
Fam	4	3. Marital separation	65
Soc	4	4. Jail term	63
Fam	4	5. Death of close family member	63

EPB ARENA	EPB Scale		Stress Points
Phy	3	6. Personal injury or illness	53
Fam	3	7. Marriage	50
Car	3	8. Fired at work	47
Fam	3	9. Marital reconciliation	45
Car	3	10. Retirement	45
Fam	3	11. Change in health of family member	44
Fam	3	12. Pregnancy	40
Sex	2	13. Sex difficulties	39
Fam	2	14. Gain of new family member	39
Car	2	15. Business readjustment	39
Car	2	16. Change in financial state	38
Soc	2	17. Death of close friend	37
Car	2	18. Change to different line of work	36
Fam	2	19. Change in number of arguments with spouse	35
Fam	2	20. Mortgage over $10,000	31
Fam	2	21. Foreclosure of mortgage or loan	30
Car	2	22. Change in responsibilities at work	29
Fam	2	23. Son or daughter leaving home	29
Fam	2	24. Troubles with in-laws	29
Per	2	25. Outstanding personal achievement	28
Fam	2	26. Spouse begins or stops work	26
Acad	2	27. Begin or end school	26
Per	2	28. Change in living conditions	25
Per	2	29. Revision of personal habits	24
Car	2	30. Trouble with boss	23
Car	2	31. Change in work hours or conditions	20
Per	2	32. Change in residence	20
Acad	2	33. Change in schools	20
Soc	1	34. Change in recreation	19
Spir	1	35. Change in church activities	19
Soc	1	36. Change in social activities	18
Fam	1	37. Mortgage or loan less than $10,000	17
Per	1	38. Change in sleeping habits	16
Fam	1	39. Change in number of family get-togethers	15
Per	1	40. Change in eating habits	15
Fam	1	41. Vacation	13
Fam	1	42. Christmas	12
Soc	1	43. Minor violations of the law	11

Total

* Modified Holmes-Rahe Social Readjustment Scale

Complete the three items below by circling the number that best represents your belief of how your daughter or son would respond.

1.   Life is a series of:

1	2	3	4	5	6	7	8	9	10

Challenges to be met   Obstacles to be avoided

2.   I have made a commitment to what I am doing:

1	2	3	4	5	6	7	8	9	10

Very Strong   Very Weak

3.   What happens in my life is mostly a result of:

1	2	3	4	5	6	7	8	9	10

Decisions I make   Chance, Fate

Enter the Stress level number (1-5) you selected from the EPB Scale for each item (1-43) on the EPB Worksheet on the following page. For example, 'Change in schools' rated #1 would be placed in the Academic Studies and Studies Related arena. So you would enter #33 in the Academic Studies arena at level #1.

A total on the Holmes-Rahe scale of 300+ points means your child is under considerable situational stress and is vulnerable to illness and/or injury. Extra measures should be taken to care for themselves. Getting adequate sleep, eating well-balanced meals, spending time with people who like them and whom they like, completing assignments on time, completing responsibilities already committed to, avoiding additional stressful undertakings, and treating themselves with kindness and caring will help them to cope more effectively until the situational stress subsides.

Another indicator of how well they cope with stress can be deduced from the responses you gave to the three questions using the 1-10 scale. Research conducted on persons with stressful lifestyles found individuals who look at life as a challenge, make commitments to what they are doing, and view what happens in their lives as a result of decisions they make suffer fewer adverse effects from stress than individuals responding on the other end of the continuum. Common sense dictates that being on either extreme all the time can create unnecessary stress. A lifestyle approach in the 4-6 range on most issues and greater intensity in the 1-3 range on issues of top priority, value, or interest may provide a more satisfying and healthier life.

By now you may have noticed that this book has emphasized that your child's success in college and in life is a result of their taking responsibility for decisions and their consequences, for believing in themselves and others as competent and caring human beings, for putting energy and commitment into the things they decide to do, and for shifting their perspectives to see more of life as a challenge to be excited about than as an obstacle to be avoided. So in addition to being successful in what they decide to do, utilizing the expanding perceptual boundaries process will result in effective stress management.

EPB Worksheet
Social Readjustment

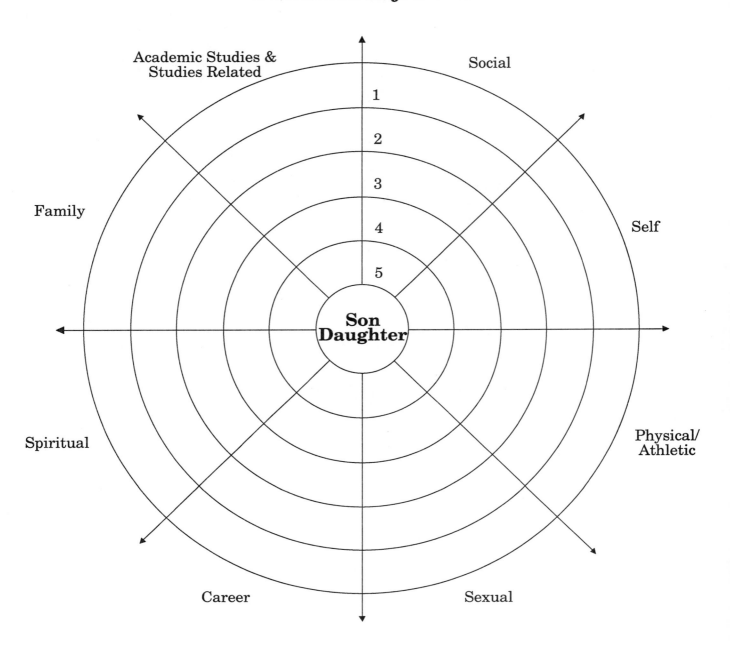

Academic Studies &
Studies Related

Social

1
2
3
4
5

Family

Self

**Son
Daughter**

Spiritual

Physical/
Athletic

Career

Sexual

DATE _____

SOME IRRATIONAL BELIEFS*

Several powerful, irrational, and illogical ideas stand in the way of our leading anxiety-free, unhostile, assertive lives.

<u>Irrational Idea #1.</u> It is a dire necessity for an adult to be loved or approved of by almost everyone for virtually everything he/she does.**

AWFULIZING THOUGHT: I WILL BE ALONE AND FRIENDLESS.

<u>Irrational Idea #2.</u> One should be thoroughly competent, adequate, and achieving in all possible respects.**

AWFULIZING THOUGHT: I'M NO GOOD

<u>Irrational Idea #3.</u> Certain people are bad, wicked or villainous and they should be severely blamed and punished for their sins. (salesclerks, mechanics, lawyers).

AWFULIZING THOUGHT: I MUST ALWAYS BE ON GUARD, AND GET THEM EVERY CHANCE I GET

<u>Irrational Idea #4.</u> It is terrible, horrible, and catastrophic when things are not going the way one would like them to go.

AWFULIZING THOUGHT: THIS IS THE WAY IT WILL BE FOREVER.

<u>Irrational Idea #5.</u> Human unhappiness is externally caused and people have little or no ability to control their sorrows or rid themselves of their negative feelings.**

AWFULIZING THOUGHT: I WILL BE TOTALLY RESPONSIBLE FOR HURTING THEIR FEELINGS.

<u>Irrational Idea #6.</u> If something is or may be dangerous or fearsome, one should be terribly occupied with and upset about it.

AWFULIZING THOUGHT: IF I FORGET ABOUT IT, IT WILL SNEAK UP AND OVERCOME ME.

<u>Irrational Idea #7.</u> It is easier to avoid facing many life difficulties and self-responsibilities than to undertake more rewarding forms of self-discipline.**

AWFULIZING THOUGHT: IT WOULD BE TERRIBLE TO ROCK THE BOAT.

<u>Irrational Idea #8.</u> The past is all-important and because something once strongly affected one's life, it should indefinitely do so.

AWFULIZING THOUGHT: I TRIED THIS ONCE AND IT
DIDN'T WORK.

<u>Irrational Idea #9.</u> People and things should be different from the way they are, and it is catastrophic if perfect solutions to the grim realities of life are not immediately found.

AWFULIZING THOUGHT: THEY SHOULD KNOW BETTER -- IT'S
NOT FAIR.   I'VE GOT TO BE ABLE TO
CHANGE THINGS TO SUIT ME OR
I'LL FALL APART.

<u>Irrational Idea #10.</u> Maximum human happiness can be achieved by inertia and inaction or by passively and committedly 'enjoying oneself'.

AWFULIZING THOUGHT: THE WAY TO BE HAPPY IS JUST TO
WAIT FOR IT. THIS ISN'T THE RIGHT
MOMENT. I'LL KNOW WHEN IT
COMES BECAUSE IF I TRY
SOMETHING ACTIVE I MIGHT FAIL.

**Most commonly used.
*From Ellis, Albert; Harper, Robert A. A Guide to Rational Living.
Wilshire Book Company, North Hollywood, CA, 1970.*

PERSONAL RIGHTS

**Right to refuse requests without having to feel guilty or selfish.

**Right to express my feelings, including anger, as long as I don't violate the rights of others; and to experience the consequences.

**Right to be competitive and achieve.

**Right to have my needs be as important as the needs of other people.

**Right to decide which activities will fulfill my needs.

**Right to make mistakes and be responsible for them.

**Right to have one's opinions given the same respect and consideration that other people's opinions are given.

**Right to change my mind.

**Right to be treated as a capable human adult and taken seriously.

**Right to be independent.

**Right to say "I don't know" and "I don't understand".

**Right to get what I pay for.

**Right to ask for information from professionals.

**Right to decide when to be assertive.

**Add you own...

I AM RESPONSIBLE FOR MYSELF. I HAVE THE RESPONSIBILITY TO RECOGNIZE THAT EVERYONE ELSE HAS THESE SAME RIGHTS.

TIME MANAGEMENT

Time management is related to stress management. If your child does not manage time effectively, they soon will feel the stress of being unprepared for tests, facing next-day deadlines for major projects, rushing to appointments they are late for, alienating or disappointing friends, and losing jobs. In general, they wind up falling 'behind' and 'behind', and not feeling good about themselves as competent adults because they are not accomplishing what they had hoped to accomplish.

An important aspect of time management, which was discussed when they set up their study schedules, was their need for some reasonable balance of academic, social, physical, spiritual, and personal activities in their lives. Activities did not have to occur every day in each arena or be given equal time. Instead the time spent in the different arenas depended on their needs and interests and available time. Look at their weekly schedules. What are they having difficulty sticking to? What adjustments did they make last week? Are they working? How do they feel when they manage time effectively? Discuss their schedules and their ability to manage time with them.

One thing that often comes out in discussions around how well we manage time, is feeling guilty for not doing our work or worrying about what test, paper, etc. is due next. The following story illustrates these points.

PAST	PRESENT	FUTURE
Guilt	*Action*	*Worry*

Let's all go to a typical weekend party at WMU. But, before we go, let's look in on Jane and her roommates, Sally and Pam. Jane has a major paper due Monday, and like many first year students, needs almost the entire weekend to get it completed because she hasn't started it yet. She told Pam and Sally that, under no circumstances, would she party this weekend. While Pam and Sally are getting ready for the party, Jane is at her desk leafing disheartedly through research books and making notes. Of course, she hears about all the neat people who will be at the party. Just before Pam and Sally are to leave, Mark, a young man Jane likes very much, calls saying he and some friends will be at the party and he is hoping to see Jane there. Jane says she has to work on "this stupid paper" and hangs up shortly. But within two minutes she throws her pen on the desk and exclaims, "There's no sense in my staying here. I won't be able to concentrate on this paper knowing you are having a good time and Mark is going to be there. I'm going with you!"

At the party, you can guess what Jane kept thinking and talking about. She felt *guilty* for having left her paper undone and not keeping the commitment she had made to herself. She *worried* about whether or not she would be able to complete the entire paper and if she couldn't, how much it might hurt her grade to hand it in late. During the entire party, it seemed Jane was either feeling guilty or worrying most of the time. Guilt is based on past behaviors and worry on future behaviors. *The only time when we ever accomplish anything or enjoy ourselves is in the present.* Yet, most of you will spend more time in the past - feeling guilty -- or in the future - feeling worried -- than you will in the present, feeling whatever feelings are appropriate for what you are doing. Check it out for yourself if you don't think so!

So if time management is a problem, don't worry about it or feel guilty--do something about it. Start living in the present. Every time this next week you notice yourself feeling guilty or worried, stop yourself, get into the present, and do something. This is also very effective at reducing test taking anxiety. Next week we'll see how successful you have been at implementing this simple, yet effective time management technique.

As a parent you may be wondering just how common such a scenario is. Without fail virtually ever student I have ever taught or counseled identifies immediately with the students in the above story. They have also reported that it really works for them to *'get in the present'* when they find themselves worrying or feeling guilty. Use this technique for yourself as well as sharing it with your daughter or son.

ACADEMIC ADVISING, MAJORS, AND CAREER CHOICE- A FEW THOUGHTS

If you have been reading and working on a chapter a week in this text, it is now early October. Soon course schedules for winter semester will be available and your child will register the first week of November.

For many students, especially those with no career direction, without a major, or who want to change majors, this can be a stressful time. They can reduce the stress and use this time as an opportunity to assess where they are in their academic and career paths and where they wish to go. This requires thinking, planning and intelligently using university resources. The following guidelines will be helpful and are written directly to your son or daughter so you can copy the page and send it to them! If they have a copy of the *Expanding Perceptual Boundaries* text they already have this information and just need to talk with you about their plans.

1.   MAKE AN APPOINTMENT WITH YOUR ACADEMIC ADVISOR TODAY! The advice of friends can be helpful yet often friends aren't familiar with requirements in a major, changes in departmental or university requirements, the diversity of offerings at WMU, or your skills, interests, values, etc. Since academic advisors get very busy this time of year, call your college (Business, Arts and Sciences, Fine Arts, Education, Health and Human Services, and

Engineering and Applied Sciences) today for an appointment. If you are in the Honors program call the Honors College and if you have not yet selected a major, call the University Curriculum advising office.

2.   **BEFORE** your appointment with an advisor, review General Education and major and minor requirements in the *University Bulletin*. Write down courses you think you must take or are interested in taking. Don't just take classes you aren't interested in in order 'to get them out of the way'. This can make for an uninspiring semester and doesn't help you narrow your curriculum and career choices.

Now pick up a course schedule and circle those classes you selected. On the schedule planning page create an initial listing of courses for winter. Pick two additional classes as alternatives in case you are closed out of some of your first choices. Check these courses with the descriptions in the *Bulletin* to see if they are what you want. If you desire more information on a particular course, call the departmental office and ask to speak to the professor or check with the secretary (stop by and ask the secretary if you may see the course syllabus). Write down any questions you wish to ask your advisor.

3.   **THINK** about how your course selection relates to your values, skills, and interests. Do you see your courses leading to a major and eventual career? Since 25% of the first year students are undecided about a major and by the time seniors graduate most have changed majors twice or more, don't feel alone or badly if you haven't yet decided what you want to do with the rest of your life!

Western has excellent resources to aid you in your career and major selection. Testing services offers the Career Test Battery, the Placement Office has job information on resume writing and interviewing, and the Counseling Center has a career media center and career counseling. Call them or stop in for a visit.

In addition, A&S100 (Career Development and Exploration) can help you to clarify your career direction. You may not choose a major but you can make significant progress in understanding the career decision-making process.

As you more clearly understand your skills, competencies, values and interests you become better able to match curriculums and careers to who you are. This step, *self-awareness and assessment, is the first* of four steps in the career process. Chickering's Developmental Tasks for College Students (Chapter Six) will help you more clearly see why this step must come first if good career and major selection are to occur.

The *second step is career awareness and exploration* and the resources mentioned above will be helpful to you in finding out about all aspects of careers from entry level education and experience requirements to pay and fringe benefits.

The *third step is decision making.* Most first year students are anxious about making the 'right' career and major choice and want to rush the process. Yet time spent on steps one and two is time well spent when you reach step three. You will now be able to make an intelligent decision based on accurate, timely, and relevant information. Oh, by the way, don't expect to feel 'absolutely sure' about your choice. The best decisions most of us make are made with some uncertainty.

Step four, planning and placement, is the time to implement your decision. The Placement Office can be a tremendous support at this time and they recommend you start a placement credentials file a year to a year and a half before you graduate.

4.   BE ON TIME for your appointment with your academic advisor. You may only have one-half hour so bring all your materials with you. This shows the advisor that you have been thinking about course selection and are actively involved in planning your future. Ask the questions you want and consider scheduling an appointment at a later date if you wish more time. Advisors can be valuable resource people so get to know them.

5.   FOLLOW DIRECTIONS FOR PHONE REGISTRATION
Enlist the aid of your classmates or an upperclass student and remember to have all your information at your fingertips. Best wishes!

Chapter 5 - EPB Mind Stretchers

1.   What are the four major strategies for coping with stress?
2.   What is the main idea of the section on time management?
3.   How can frequent abuse of alcohol be related to stress?
4.   Muscle relaxation and acting assertively are strategies to change your response to a stressful situation. How do they differ?
5.   How can you realistically create a less stressful environment for yourself and support your child in doing likewise?
6.   What do you think it will mean for your son or daughter personally if they live more in the present than in the past or future?

SUCCESS TRIAD SUMMARY
Chapter 5 - Stress Management

CHALLENGES:

1. Understand the nature of the stress in their lives and take appropriate steps to reduce stress.
2. Prevent or minimize some of the symptoms of stress by getting adequate rest, exercising, and eating well-balanced meals.
3. Feel more in control of their lives by keeping their word, not procrastinating, thinking positively of themselves and others, and developing the skills necessary to be successful in life.
4. Budget time realistically with an eye toward balancing life's demands and opportunities.
5. Plan their academic program for next term with a college advisor.
6. Learn to live more in the present instead of worrying (future) or feeling guilty (past).

SUPPORT:

1. Possibly purchase for them time management or stress reduction aids.
2. In October when stress takes its toll of students in terms of visits to the Health Center and Counseling Center, send a gift package of Vitamin C's, orange juice, treats, cards etc.

CARING:

1. Encourage them to talk openly with you about the stresses they are experiencing.
2. Make them aware of the impact of stress in October and encourage them to get more sleep and take good care of themselves during this period.
3. Help them to brainstorm then problem-solve different responses to reduce stress.
4. Be aware of and make efforts to reduce non-productive stress in your parent-child interactions (ex. criticizing them, not showing confidence in them, having unrealistic academic, career, or athletic expectations of them).
5. Replace non-productive parent-child interactions with positive, validating, stress reducing interactions (believe in them and their abilities, respect their views, point out their strengths, encourage them to take health enhancing risks, let them know you love them etc.).

Chapter Six
Self - Concept

SELF-CONCEPT AND IDENTITY

The best resource available to us as we deal with life's challenges and opportunities is 'me'. The stronger this 'me' is, the more effectively we will be able to live a productive and happy life. Making 'me' stronger is a process of expanding the perceptual boundaries of 'self'. You can be a great support to your daughter or son in this expansion even if your previous interactions interfered with the expansion of their 'me' boundary. The important step is to commit to behaviors that are growth enhancing for your child and, therefore, for yourself.

The material in this chapter and the 'Vultures' and 'UFAIRE' exercises that follow will allow you to define your son's or daughter's 'self' boundaries, understand how they are maintained, and begin the work of boundary expansion. Chickering's Developmental Tasks of the College Student and Perry's Cognitive Model are models of the growth issues your child will be experiencing while at Western; issues that will be experienced more successfully if their self-concept is strong.

SELF-CONCEPT

These are some of the important concepts and ideas that are accepted about self and self-concept.

- Your own self-concept includes your beliefs and feelings about who and what you are.

- Your behavior, at any given time, is the result of your self-concept at the moment of your behavior.

- Your self-concept is like a montage made up of many different images of your beliefs and feelings about yourself.

- No one is born with a self-concept fully formed; it develops as a result of your perception of life experiences.

- Perceptions are the actual meanings, interpretations, or judgments you make regarding your experiences and yourself.

- Perceptions are based upon the meanings individuals assign to experiences rather than on verifiable facts.

- The 'ideal self' is the vision you have of yourself as you would like to be.

- Your self-concept can be realistic or unrealistic, positive or negative, broad or narrow.

- You are now responsible for what you believe and feel about yourself.

- A person with a healthy, adequate, positive, self-concept is likely to take risks, to develop new competencies, to explore new experiences.

- Once formed, you tend to interpret yourself and your experiences in ways consistent with your existing self-concept.

- With a deep desire to change, a willingness to risk, and a willingness to seek out positive experiences, you are capable of changing your concept to make it more realistic, more adequate, and more positive.

From: *"Self-Concept: How I Know Who I Am,"* **Sunburst Communications, 1982.**

CHICKERING'S DEVELOPMENTAL TASKS OF THE COLLEGE STUDENT

Chickering has identified seven interdependent tasks that your son or daughter will be working to complete while in college. Somewhat comparable to Maslow's needs hierarchy, Chickering's tasks require successful completion (not perfection!) of the previous task to move to the next task with a good chance of success.

The **first** task, **Developing Competence**, is why most students are attending college; to increase their skills intellectually, physically, socially, and interpersonally so they are capable of completing a wide range of academic, social, or career tasks. Course work, athletic teams, intramurals, clubs, organizations, part-time jobs, informal gatherings with friends, parties, volunteer work all provide opportunities to develop new and enhance existing skills. Again the value of a well-rounded education balancing academic, physical, personal, and social development is evident. Confidence in their ability to be successful increases as they complete this task.

The **second** task, **Managing Emotions**, requires that they increase their awareness of feelings and integrate these feelings appropriately into their lives. This is easier to do with a sense of self-confidence acquired from completing task one. This confidence coupled with an increasing awareness of a wide range of emotions will help them establish the flexible control and expression of feelings characteristic of a mature responsible adult instead of the more rigid or explosive expression of feelings characteristic of the adolescent. More than eighteen years of working with students has convinced me of the difficulty of this task and its importance to successful relationships as well as stress reduction. Our society has not particularly valued a healthy display of emotions, especially in men, and learning this important behavior with few role models is very difficult. If your son or daughter has difficulty expressing feelings (as opposed to thoughts) personal counseling might prove beneficial. The investment of time and energy is worth it, for being able to express emotions appropriately is a life-long skill that enhances our work, personal, and social life.

The **third** task, **Developing Autonomy,** requires your daughter or son to use what they have learned in tasks one and two. In order to decrease their dependence, move toward greater self-directedness, and recognize their interdependence on others and their environment, they will need well-developed competencies and mature handling of emotions. This is a complex task that leads to a greater sense of responsibility for all their actions and a realignment of their rights and freedoms.

This task most directly affects their relationship with you. When younger they had relatively little freedom and few rights or responsibilities. As your child aged these should have increased based on their ability to handle them (tasks 1&2). Primary responsibility for them still resided with you as parents. Now the balance has shifted. This is not a clear break with parents but a recognition that they are growing into young adults. They have more freedom and more rights than they have had before and with them comes more responsibility for all their actions. At first this can be uncomfortable for you and your children, but it is essential if they are to take their place as a mature, responsible, confident, and happy member of society. How often have you heard people complain that young people are irresponsible! Responsibility cannot be dictated to young people. They must learn it by being challenged appropriately to take on new tasks and to be accountable for the consequences. *Warning!* Parents who attempt to over-control their children, restrict their growth, and therefore interfere with the successful completion of this task may see no improvement in their relationship with their child, or worse, may experience a deterioration of that relationship because the young adult knows they must go against the parents' wishes if they are to grow. What a double bind for a child! Good communication, expressions of confidence in your child, and encouragement and cooperation in the growth process are needed.

Successful completion of this task leads to the most pivotal task, number **four, Establishing Identity**. Identity refers to the development of a consistent sense of who you are and a match (congruence) between your own view of yourself and other's view of you. This does not mean you are what others think but that you act as a competent, emotionally mature, responsible person and others see you this way also. One way to think of identity is to picture each human being as a filtering and processing unit. We are all exposed to millions of stimuli from words to dust particles, from behaviors to feelings which we filter, process, and react to. The healthier our personal identity, the more durable this filter, the better we filter out that which is harmful to us and process productively that which is healthy for us and contributes to our growth. I have worked with too many college students as well as older adults who, due to a weak, unhealthy sense of identity and a weak self-concept, take in and believe so many toxic things about themselves that they feel totally unworthy as human beings. Besides the individual tragedy, as a society and world we cannot afford the wasting away of so much human potential.

Establishing identity is pivotal because it depends upon accomplishment of the previous three tasks while the remaining three depend upon the establishment of a sound sense of identity.

The **fifth** task, **Freeing Interpersonal Relationships**, is represented by increased tolerance and acceptance of differences between individuals and an increased capacity for mature and intimate relationships. Perhaps now you can understand why so many of your son's or daughter's relationships were often stressful and growth limiting. Having relationships based on understanding, openness, honesty, and trust requires individuals who have been willing to take the risks and go through the discomfort of the previous tasks to gain the satisfaction of truly healthy interpersonal relationships. Therefore, your commitment to work to support your child's accomplishment of Chickering's tasks is an investment in them, their relationships with others, and of most importance to parents, their relationship with you.

The **sixth** task, **Developing Purpose**, is successfully completed when they have a career direction and clear lifestyle preference that is well integrated with their identity. For many students much or most of the first and second years are needed to get a clear enough sense of identity to make good curriculum, major, minor, and career decisions. Late sophomore to early junior year is often the time many students declare majors and feel more of a commitment to a particular career. You may be thinking that they should know what they want to do by the time they get to college and become worried that your child doesn't know and all others do! The facts are that more students than ever before are entering college without a declared major, they are taking five years on average to graduate, they are declaring majors later, and 75% will change their major twice or more. To pressure students into premature major and career decisions may alleviate some parental anxiety about your child wasting money and time but more often it can result in an inappropriate choice which gets more costly to correct, a loss of motivation, and sometimes even results in dropping out of school by disenchanted students.

Universities are investing more resources in career support services for students. Encourage your son or daughter to contact the career counselors in the Counseling Center. They will work with your child to make good major and career decisions and can help them to complete any unfinished developmental tasks needed to make appropriate career choices. They may also refer your daughter or son to Testing Services to take the excellent Career Test Battery, to Placement Services for interviewing or resume writing practice, to the Career Development class (AS 100), to the Career Media Center or Library for current information on careers and majors as well as interactive computer programs which aid in career decision making.

The **seventh** task, **Developing Integrity**, is represented by a personalized set of values, a shifting away from the absoluteness of authority, and a congruence between your son's or daughter's values and their behavior. You will notice success in this task when they more often than not resist peer pressure or parental pressure to do things that violate their beliefs or values and act on things they believe in and value even though others may not be pleased or approve. As you can well imagine this can result in despair or joy for parents! If you have worked through this book with your child, I believe you will be able to accept the choices your son or daughter makes more readily than parents who have not taken the time to understand their child's needs.

I want to share a personal experience that I had and you may be feeling after reading this section. I realized that I had not satisfactorily completed all of Chickering's tasks when I was in college and that many of them I hadn't made real progress on until I was in my 30's! If you are thinking this also, you have a lot of company. Because these developmental issues were left too much to chance while we were growing-up, most adults with college aged students find themselves lacking the skills, attitudes, and behaviors to be as helpful to their son or daughter as they would like to be.

So what can you do? Talk openly to your child about what you learned and didn't learn when you were young and how you feel inadequate at times to do the best that can be done for them. The more open you are the less likely it is that your limitations will become those of your child. If you aren't open with them, you will tend not to help them grow in areas where you, yourself, are uncomfortable. Unfortunately for your daughter or son this may limit them the rest of their lives as it has you. So for your child's growth be willing to look honestly and openly at your strengths and limitations and commit to your own growth. If you are not willing to take the risks and experience the discomfort necessary to expand your own boundaries, at least tell this to your child and encourage them to grow and be all they can be.

Successful completion of all of Chickering's Tasks will take your child's and your commitment to their growth, and a willingness to be uncomfortable. Their increased sense of career, academic, and interpersonal competence and self-confidence and the understanding and respect evident in their relationship with you will be worth the effort. It will also enable them to progress more rapidly through Perry's model for cognitive development.

PERRY'S COGNITIVE MODEL

Like Chickering, Perry's work with college students resulted in his awareness that students progressed in a developmental way to more complex ways of thinking.

Perry proposed that first year students tend to be dualistic thinkers. Things are black or white, professors have the answers and students don't, so they should tell them. Dualists are often threatened by those who think differently and miss out on learning because they tend to label so much of it 'wrong' and therefore not worthy of learning. Dualists also tend to group people as good or bad, friend or foe, and can be very intolerant and unaccepting. Have you noticed this in the comments your daughter or son makes about classes or social interactions?

Often perceived threat and stress can keep first year students in a dualistic stage. The more they work to expand their boundaries, build their self-confidence, and progress thru Chickering's developmental tasks the easier it will be for them to move from dualism to the multiplistic stage.

Multiplists realize knowledge is not absolute and that there are areas of grey. Grey, however, is the exception and most knowledge is black or white if they can just find out which. They can get frustrated with professors or parents who hide the truth and make them work to find it.

Relativists represent the next stage and have learned that grey, in fact, is the rule and there is little absolute knowledge. In classes, they often think their opinion is as correct as the professor's since most everything is grey, but they often haven't done the research or critical thinking to support their views. Generally, they are comfortable with the grey, but will retreat to a multiplistic or even dualistic way of thinking if the greyness overwhelms them; if there is too much stress.

So the process of expanding perceptual boundaries also helps support their progress through Perry's cognitive model by helping them to feel less stressed and threatened by the grey in the world. As their boundaries expand in all of the different life arenas their capacity to benefit from, understand and enjoy the richness of life, which is often in the grey areas, will also increase.

IMPROVE YOUR SELF-CONCEPT

You are a unique, creative, talented, competent, warm, caring human being worthy of respect, understanding, love, and acceptance. **STOP.** Do you think this description is of someone else? Did you read the above description going, "Not me. If only you knew what I was really like!" If so, you have just identified areas where your self-concept needs rebuilding. Self-concept is your appraisal or evaluation of yourself and is the single biggest factor determining your success and happiness in life. It is an evaluation influenced by the physical environment, social climate, friends, loved ones, and yourself. This evaluation is not only experienced in the form of a conscious, verbalized judgment but, also, as a feeling, a feeling that is part of every other feeling.

"The nature of your self-evaluation has a profound effect on your thinking processes, emotions, desires, values, and goals. It is the single most significant key to your behavior." (Branden, 1969)

A healthy self-concept makes successful completion of Chickering's and Perry's tasks more likely. The most disturbing research I have read, reported that a child's self-concept actually gets worse the more years they spend in the educational system! This is a travesty. Self-concept should expand and get stronger as we grow, not get weaker. How can young people grow into healthy and successful adults if they don't like themselves? And how can this country expect to produce quality products and services if the people doing the work are so internally weak?

At the college level there is tremendous work that needs to be done to enhance the self-concept of our students if we expect them to reach excellence; to reach their potential. When honest and thoughtful effort is applied to supporting the enhancement of their self-concept students respond beautifully. They report feeling more confident, being more successful, taking more risks to expand their boundaries, and working more cooperatively with others. Let's take a look at how your child's self-concept got to be what it is today and what they and you can do to enhance their self-concept.

Vultures

Your daughter or son was born into this world with an intact self-concept, one needing to develop and grow, yet one without negative attachments. However, as they grew, they began to have doubts about themselves, about their competence and perhaps even their worth as a human being. Some doubts came from negative experiences in their life. Many of these doubts came from criticisms from parents, siblings, or close friends. As parents, no one is perfect and we all have done things to damage the self-concept of our children as well as things to enhance it. Your present and future contribution to the success and happiness of your child is not to get defensive about what was done in the past but to make a commitment to put energy into helping your child grow. By the way, most of the negative thoughts you have about yourself can be traced back to early learnings from your parents or other influential persons in your life. Blame at this point is useless. What is needed is the assumption of responsibility for your self-concept and a commitment to make the changes you desire. The same assumption is needed by your daughter or son but you can contribute to making the process somewhat easier and certainly quicker.

Though often subtle and/or unintentional, these criticisms from such important people in their lives were internalized by them into negative self-thoughts and feelings. Let's call these psychological self-put-downs 'vultures'. (Simon, 1977) Every time they 'do' a vulture, they take a hunk out of their self-concept. If they do many vultures in a day (and most students do hundreds), their self-concept is pretty weak by evening, too weak to deal successfully with the challenges and stresses they face in college. Vultures are done in all eight EPB life arenas. These are listed below with examples. See how many vultures you can identify for your child. Then try it for yourself. You're worth it.

1. **Physical/Athletic** - "I'm fat and nobody worthwhile would want to associate with someone so unworthy". "Her hair is so beautiful, I wish I had hair like her's instead of this rat's nest".

2. **Academic/Studies Related** - "I'm so stupid. I could never pass that math course". "If I don't get an "A" in every course, Mom and Dad will know I'm not too bright".

3. **Social** - "I'd really like to meet him, but I'm so boring he'd never like me". "She wouldn't go out with somebody like me. She only dates _____ ".(fill in the blank).

4. **Family** - "Damn! Forgot Mom and Dad's anniversary. What kind of a no-good son am I anyway"? "My sister is such a great athlete. I know I'm a disappointment to my parents because I'm not".

5. **Career** - "Who would hire me for a job? I have nothing to offer".

6. **Self** - "I'm not as good as other people. There are so many things about myself that I don't like. I'm just not as important as they are".

7. **Spiritual** - "I don't believe everything about my religion anymore. I feel lost and think I'm a bad person".

8. **Sexual** - "I'm not sexually endowed like the women (men) in all the magazines. Therefore, I'll probably be inadequate sexually". "I'm not sexually attractive as I am so I better buy this _____ (fill in a product such as toothpaste, perfume, etc.). otherwise, everyone will know how inadequate I am".

Notice the negative self-appraisal characteristic of vultures. It is important to recognize that this negative self-appraisal is not based on facts. Just because your son or daughter is overweight or forgot your anniversary, does not mean they are a bad or unworthy person. If they wish to change their behavior, fine, they should then do so, but they don't need to put negative labels on themselves.

Look over the eight arenas and identify the self-put-downs your son or daughter does in each. List them. Realize you may not be aware of many of them so I hope you will take the time to sit down with your child and go over *your perception* of the vultures they do and get *their perception*. Then my hope is you and they will commit to saying and doing that which will enhance their self-concept.

You may wonder how helpful is it for them to keep doing vultures? Don't we all need to be self-critical and criticized by others. No. Emphatically no! Only a small percentage of people grow when frequently criticized and they do so with a rebellious "I'll show you" attitude seeped in anger and hostility. Instead most people learn to doubt themselves, their abilities, and their basic worth upon receiving so many negatives relative to the positives they receive and accept. I know students that cannot and will not accept a compliment because they don't believe they deserve it. This is a tragedy. How do we expect people to be productive and happy when we have told them all their lives how bad they are. People like plants need nourishment and a healthy environment to optimize their growth. Criticism is like poison to most of us and you should do everything possible to minimize the criticism you do of anyone, including yourself and especially your children. An honest and open discussion of this section can begin a new and positive chapter in your relationship with your child and perhaps yourself, spouse, and others.

Let's see how you can eliminate or minimize the vultures and enhance self-concept instead of tearing it apart.

In doing presentations on vultures and self-concept for over ten years with more than 3,000 people, 99.9 percent of these people admitted doing vultures in all eight arenas. So look around. All those super people you think don't have any self-concept problems are doing vultures just like you and your children are. You are not alone. We are all in it together.(While in college I used to believe I was the only one with so many negative self-thoughts)

Three approaches to enhancing self-concept will be described. They are: (1) stopping the negative thoughts, (2) self and other validation, and (3) being a doer.

Thought Stopping

Vultures are negative thoughts about yourself based on beliefs learned early in life. These beliefs have been internalized and used to weaken how you feel and think about yourself. You can begin to repair your self-concept by being aware of your vultures and stopping the thoughts. If the negative thought is well under way, finish it and add a positive action statement. Be sure the positive statement is one that you can achieve. For example: "I've gained five pounds. Am I a slob! Wait a minute, I have gained five pounds so I'll cut back on sweets and play some tennis until the weight is where I want it". There is no reason to put yourself down for gaining the weight. Also, stop name calling such as "hippo", "thunder thighs", "bird brain", or "stupid".

Validation

Validation, whether by yourself or others, is the process of recognizing who you are and where you belong. Ultimately, it is your evaluation, not the conclusions of others, that counts most because it is you who decides to accept or reject the evaluations of others. For students who grew up having learned to listen to authority, do what they were told, not to do anything embarrassing, please their parents and teachers, and needing the acceptance and approval of friends it is difficult for them to believe their own evaluation of themselves is more important than anyone else's.

Self-validation is the process of recognizing their good qualities (their skills, values, interests, beliefs, feelings, thoughts, physical attributes, and behaviors) and taking credit for them. This does not mean that they are oblivious of their weaker points, but that they should focus in on their strengths. Remember, they are working to build up their self-concept, not tear it down. Unfortunately, all too often they have been taught to look at their shortcomings, to accept criticism, and embrace their weaknesses. But if they mentioned their strengths they were bragging; they were told they needed to be more humble. *Garbage!* The emotional and physical price paid in this country for that type of thinking is phenomenal. Think for a minute. Are you happier when dwelling on what a bad person you are or when recognizing that you are a good person? And when do you feel more productive or more like reaching out to others? When you feel good about yourself, of course. How do you think this works for your child?

Jean Houston, a researcher on human potential, has said most people function at 10 percent of their potential! One reason is they don't believe in themselves. They'll turn away a compliment yet believe a criticism. Does this make any sense? The irony is that while they are doing all they can to destroy their self-concept, they expect to be happy and productive. Life doesn't work that way. You are responsible for your happiness and productivity and can affect both by being a lot kinder to yourself. The same is true for your daughter or son. **Be POSITIVE, POSITIVE, POSITIVE!**

Validation from others is important also. Much of the validation received from important others was lost when they enrolled at Western. In a previous chapter, 'Loneliness', it was pointed out how removal of most sources of validation can contribute to loneliness and how important it was to make contact with others, to develop a social network. Research has shown that people with positive self-concepts find it easier to make friends and to adjust to being in college.

Be aware, however, that not all the people your son or daughter calls friends or acquaintances are good for their self-concept. Do you know people that when you are with them, you don't feel good about yourself, you feel emotionally drained, attacked, negative, not listened to or cared about? These people are toxic. They are poison to your self-concept and should be avoided if at all possible. Your child needs to avoid such people also.

Choose, instead, people who are nourishing. With nourishing people, they will feel good about themselves, feel more alive, full of energy, hopeful, enthusiastic, positive, and cared about. Around such people, when dealing with challenges, they will think **"I CAN"**, not "I can't". I have found more students missing out on fantastic life experiences by saying "I can"t" without making any effort whatsoever. They limit their possibilities, miss the chance to develop new competencies, and diminish their self-concept. Associating with nourishing people and being nourishing to others will enhance their willingness to risk to take advantage of life's opportunities. Described below are six pointers for having better relationships with others and positively validating themselves. Apply these to yourself and then to your child.

U - Understanding - do you understand yourself and others? Be a good listener and empathize with others. Communicate openly and honestly.

F - Forgiveness - though forgiveness seems to free the other person, it truly frees you. You pay the price for holding onto your anger and hatred. Let it go - for both your sakes.

A - Acceptance - can you see and accept yourself and others as worthy, unique, yet imperfect human beings, okay as you are? Or do you keep your distance from people by concluding they are the wrong color, race, religion, a non-athlete, etc., etc., etc.? Be accepting of yourself and others.

I - Interest - are you interested in yourself and others? Show it. Look at them when they talk. Listen to them. Tell them what you think you heard.

R - Respect - do you respect yourself and others? All people deserve respect initially - some lose it later by their actions.

E - Encouragement or Hope - times can get rough, and we all need to believe they will get better. We also need encouragement to believe in our potential; that we can do more than we sometimes think we can. Do you encourage others and are you hopeful for yourself?

At our most human level, we all want and need understanding, forgiveness, acceptance, interest, respect, and encouragement or hope. If our children are not doing these things for themselves, how can we expect them to do them for others? They can only give to others that which they have given to themselves or allowed to be given to them. Keep in mind the acronym, **U-FAIRE**. Be fair to yourself and fair to others.

Be A Doer

Your child can also enhance her/his self-concept by being a doer. People who are active participants in life get more out of it than those who sit back being passive and inactive. Set tasks or goals and accomplish them. Don't get hung up on being perfect. Perfection is a concept. Perfection has never been and never will be achieved. They aren't perfect so don't expect them to accomplish a task perfectly or achieve a goal way beyond their capacities. I've noticed a relationship between perfectionism and procrastination in many bright students. The only way they can justify not being perfect (getting 'A's) is to wait until the last minute to do their work and then state they could have gotten an 'A' if they had more time. This allows them to maintain the myth of perfectionism. It would be healthier not to procrastinate, be a doer, and live with the real consequences for their efforts instead of the neurotic belief that they could be perfect if only they put in more effort and had more time.

Since success is important, they should set up tasks or goals where they can reasonably succeed. If there is no challenge or risk, the success won't seem as sweet; their self-concept won't grow as much as when they accomplish a more challenging task. Students with particularly low self-concepts should attempt less challenging tasks until their confidence grows.

Recent research has shown outdoor adventure education programs where tasks are challenging and concrete to be the most effective strategy for enhancing self-concept. Encourage your daughter or son to participate in the activities offered through Pretty Lake Adventure Centre: rock climbing, caving, backpacking, group initiatives, ropes course, etc. Other groups like the WMU Outdoor Club, the Physical Education Department, and Honors College provide opportunities for outdoor adventures. For many adventure activities, qualified leaders are necessary. Check qualifications before going on an adventure where specialized skills are required.

Be prepared to fail. All successful people fail, but they learn from the failures. The next time they undertake a challenge, they will have a better chance of being successful. So if your son or daughter hasn't failed in a while, they probably haven't been risking enough. The idea of taking a challenge or risk will often arouse fears and anxieties and these topics will be addressed in the next chapter. For now, you can help enhance your child's self-concept by encouraging them to undertake tasks with a high probability of success and challenging them to take increasingly bigger risks by expressing your confidence in them and their ability to accomplish what they set out to do.

Summary

Self-concept is the subjective appraisal your child has of her/himself and is the best resource they will ever have to contribute to a happy and productive life. Because criticism of themselves and others is detrimental to maintaining a healthy, intact, and growing self-concept, stop the criticism and be more positive. **They are beautiful and unique. Believe it! Act on it!**

As human beings, we all have needs for understanding, forgiveness, acceptance, interest in us, respect, and encouragement or hope. Students, faculty and staff, as well as family, friends, and acquaintances can contribute positively to each other's self-concepts if we live the acronym U-FAIRE. Certainly such changes will not be easy. Risks will need to be taken.

The following quote makes an appropriate closing:

*"To venture causes anxiety, but not to venture is
to lose one's self...And to venture in the highest
sense is precisely to become conscious of one's self."*

Soren Kierkegaard

VULTURES*

The eight arenas of your life in which you do VULTURES -- psychological self-put downs. What are your childs? What are yours? Write them below.

1. **Physical/Athletic**

2. **Academic/Studies related**

3. **Social**

4. **Family**

5. **Career**

6. **Self**

7. **Spiritual**

8. **Sexual**

I commit myself to not saying the following negative things about my son or daughter because they contribute to his/her negative self-concept. Instead I wish to contribute to them developing a realistic, positive self-concept:

1.

2.

3.

4.

5.

Credit to Sidney Simon

UFAIRE
A GUIDE TO GOOD RELATIONSHIPS

U   understanding

F   forgiveness

A   acceptance

I   interest

R   respect

E   encouragement/hope

With myself, I am good at doing...
(write appropriate UFAIRE words - example - forgiveness, interest)

With myself, I want to do more...
(write appropriate UFAIRE words - example - acceptance, respect)

With my son or daughter, I am good at doing...
(write appropriate UFAIRE words - example - understanding, respect)

With my son or daughter, I want to do more...
(write appropriate UFAIRE words -example-acceptance, encouragement)

If I did UFAIRE, I would...
(complete with feeling and behavior statement)
Example: be more accepting of my son/daughter - be less critical of
his/her friends behavior and feel better about them. This would reduce
the tension I feel around them when I am being judgmental and increase
the positive things I say, feel and think about them.

94

NOTES

Chapter 6 - EPB Mind Stretchers

1. Who was responsible for the development of your child's self-concept over the past 18 years? Who is responsible now?
2. What is the main idea of the Vultures section?
3. How is negative self-talk about their academic abilities an example of limiting growth of their perceptual boundaries in the academic arena?
4. What evidence do you have that positive self-concept as opposed to a negative self-concept enhances your child's chances for being a successful person?
5. What might happen to you personally, the relationship with your son or daughter as well as with your friends if you did fewer Vultures, were more positive, and practiced UFAIRE?
6. If I were interviewing your child for a summer job and asked them to tell me ten positive things about him/herself what do you think they would say?

SUCCESS TRIAD SUMMARY
Chapter 6 - Self-Concept and Identity

CHALLENGES:

1. Establish a healthy identity by learning to minimize negative self-statements and maximize positive self-evaluations.
2. Continue the process leading to successful completion of Chickering's developmental tasks.
3. Develop higher levels of critical thinking skills as indicated in Perry's model.

SUPPORT:

1. Fund your son's or daughter's participation in activities or workshops that have a strong possibility of enhancing their sense of self-esteem.

CARING:

1. Increase the type and frequency of communications that help to enhance your child's sense of self-confidence and self-worth.
2. Model a healthy self-concept by being less self-critical and less critical of others. Be more positive about yourself, others and your involvements.
3. Encourage them to take risks that will help them grow and enhance their self-confidence.
4. Ask them questions which develop and hone their critical thinking skills.
5. Talk with them about Chickering's developmental tasks and listen to what they feel and think is happening in each stage for themselves and their friends.
6. If you think your daughter or son has such a negative self-concept that it is interfering with their success and happiness refer them for counseling. (Services of the University Counseling Center are free to students)

96

NOTES

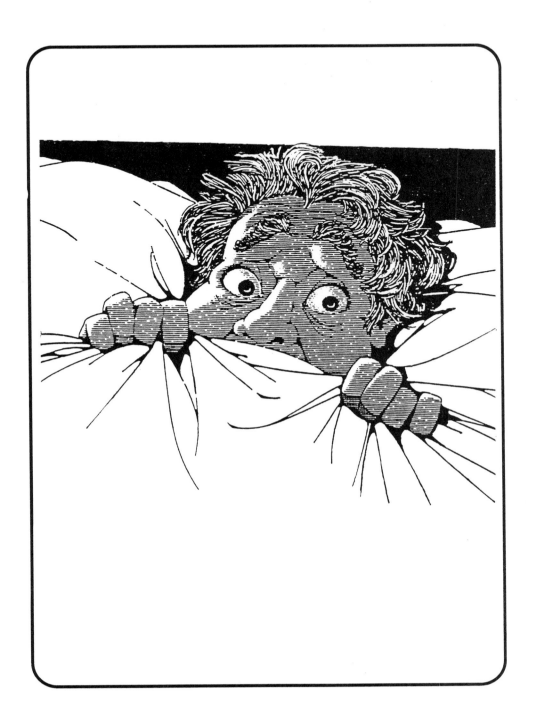

Chapter Seven
Fear and Risk-Taking

FEAR AND RISK-TAKING

Fear is a part of being alive. It is a feeling like joy or happiness (though not as pleasant) that is shared by all living things. In fact fear is a very common and potentially useful emotion. Unfortunately, fear has gotten a bad reputation due to misunderstandings and myths. Understanding how you deal with fear can open your life in exciting ways. Hopefully, your understanding will enable you to encourage your children to risk and support them when they risk in life enhancing ways.

A popular myth about fear is the myth of comfort as it relates to change. Many of you have learned not to do something if you are afraid; to wait until you are more comfortable. The misunderstanding inherent in this myth is that change in your life occurs during states of emotional comfort. The seductiveness of this belief lies in the fact that most of you would prefer to be comfortable as opposed to experiencing the discomfort, anxiety and fear that are part and parcel of significant change. So would I!

In truth, significant life changes or significant expansion of your perceptual boundaries are almost always accompanied by fear. Fear is natural when you are undertaking something where the results are unknown; where there are no guarantees of success. Keep in mind that your sons and daughters because of the nature of the college experience are confronting the unknown on a daily basis and certainly no one is giving them any guarantees of success.

It is helpful at this point to realize that no two people experience fear in exactly the same way. For example, your daughter might be afraid of talking to you about changing her major to one she knows you will disapprove of, yet her roommate may have little or no fear about such a talk with her parents. Your daughter's roommate, however, may have an extreme fear of spiders while your daughter finds spiders fascinating and has no fear of them. Because of what they have learned about themselves and their world, each of them has very individualized fears. Therefore, specific advice from others about when to risk or not to risk is often not helpful. The more you have utilized the previous material to gain a better understanding of yourself and your son or daughter the easier it will be for you to support his/her risking for growth even if it happens to be a risk you disagree with. The guideline becomes their healthy growth not your discomfort or liking of the risk.

You can help your children as well as yourself if you understand the following principles:

A)   **Comfort Myth** - Risking for change without fear is a myth. Fear is not an all-or-nothing feeling in the sense that you experience it 100 percent or 0 percent. Most often you experience different degrees of fear. If you wait until you are comfortable to risk, you probably won't take many risks necessary to be a successful and happy human being.

B)   **Degrees of Fear** - You can often decrease your level of fear before risking by working to minimize fears through rational thinking and use of facts. For example, if you are deathly afraid to sky dive, you can reduce this fear by examining the safety records of airplanes and sky divers. You will find that it is a safe sport and your extreme fear will decrease.

C)   **Safety** - Physical and emotional safety are key factors in any decision to risk - *DO TAKE* risks that promise to enhance your life and expand your boundaries. *NEVER TAKE* risks with a high probability of serious physical or emotional injury. Such risks are stupid; not brave or courageous. In times of crisis, this isn't always possible, but you will take 99 percent of your risks in non-crisis times. For example, your son might risk confronting his girlfriend about their relationship because of the chance that this talk will deepen the relationship by clearing up a bothersome issue. Of course there is the risk of the relationship deteriorating or ending. Yet he can approach her in ways to minimize the negative possibilities and increase the positive possibilities. By way of contrast, a stupid risk would be a decision to drive in a car with a driver he knows is drunk because he is afraid of his friends thinking he is weak or scared. How does such a risk enhance his life compared with the possibility of it ending his life? A risk (because he may fear their rejection), and a life enhancing risk, would be to suggest another person drive who is not drunk. Then within a day or two he could talk with his friends about having a designated driver whenever they go out to party.

D)   **Fear and Anxiety vs Hope** - Fear is a specific form of anxiety and is considered to be the most conservative force in the universe with hope as its counterbalance. Too much fear or anxiety and you behave conservatively and won't risk. In order to risk, hope of a desirable outcome must outweigh the fear of a failure. In order to help your children take life enhancing risks, you can encourage them to think positively about the end result, positively about resources (people or things) they need to accomplish their goal, and positively about themselves as competent persons who will be successful.

You can see clearly in this case the importance of successful completion of Chickering's developmental tasks.

E)   **Support** - One way to tip the balance from favoring fear and not risking, to hope and risking is to get support. People who believe in you and want to see you succeed should be sought out. Avoid those who put you down, doubt your capabilities, and don't believe in you, or don't want you to succeed. Supporters can be a great asset in your life. Students have told me repeatedly that the best support from their parents is often your belief in them and their ability to reach their goals. Such belief needs to be verbalized often and followed by encouragement. If this sounds like you are being asked to be a cheerleader for your daughter or son, you are right! Wouldn't you have loved to have your parents cheering you on, encouraging you, and believing in you every step of the way? There is also great pleasure to gain from supporting others, especially your children. Are you willing to support them so that they might take the risks necessary to live a fuller life?

F)   Fear as a Directional for Growth - As mentioned above, your son or daughter has learned many myths and has had misunderstandings with regard to fear and risk-taking that have inhibited their growth. Instead of perceiving fear as a negative to be avoided for the safer feeling of comfort, they can choose to look at fear as a signal for potentially positive change in their lives and the excitement that goes with such risks for growth. They will quickly experience the fact that fear and life enhancing risks and excitement and happiness go together. Such risking is also essential if they are to increase their sense of competence, self-confidence, and self-worth. So encourage them to look around at all the risks they can take to expand their boundaries and grow. Help them to understand how they can use fear as a positive directional to a more fulfilling life.

As you do the following exercises, keep in mind that by reducing fear by one or two levels (example EPB Level 5 to EPB Level 3), your son or daughter may have gone from experiencing fear as incapacitating to experiencing fear as uncomfortable but not so uncomfortable that they won't risk. Once they understand the process for dealing with their fears, they can generalize this learning to other life situations and increase their chances of handling those situations more effectively.

The Risking Process Chart (Figure 10) is a guide to help you understand the stages involved in all risks. For example, this is how it might work for your child: As a student you (1) experience anxiety, stomach upset, and an increased rate of breathing when you think about telling your parents you are failing Biology. You (2) want to tell them and have them still love, respect, and accept you. The (3) activity to accomplish your want is to set a time, sit down with your parents and in an adult fashion tell them you are failing Biology. You are (4) afraid your mother will compare you to your very smart sister and your father will think you goofed off and partied too much. Your deeper (4) fear is that their behavior means they don't understand you, don't respect you, don't accept you, and perhaps, don't love you. This fear would stop you from telling them except for the 'hope' you have that they will respond as loving adults and that even if they don't you are doing the right thing. Realize there is much other evidence of their love, realize they may have a perfectionist trend that you don't have to accept for yourself, and realize you have learned from your situation and have confidence you can prevent a recurrence.

You then (5) commit to telling them, leap into the unknown (their actual response and your reaction) and (6) tell them. After you (7) evaluate, you determine if you (8) achieved your goal in total, part, or not at all and make any (9) adjustments necessary, One adjustment could be a decision to deal as an adult directly and honestly with your parents.(See Chapter 9-Relationships)

Use the risking process to work through several risks you've noticed your son or daughter has avoided to date and see if you can talk this over with them as soon as possible. Hopefully, as you help them to understand the risking process and they explain why they haven't risked as of yet, they will start to shift the balance from fear and not risking to hope and risking for growth.

"The greatest risk of all is not to risk at all."

WALLS

Most of my life I've built walls.
Walls that stand strong and tall.
Walls that cannot be destroyed.
Walls that I can protect myself from all.
Walls that I can see out, but no one can see in.

Along comes someone and the walls are shaken.
Shaken to the point that I'm on the run.
Trying to resist friendship and fun.
I wish the walls within were like the sun, too bright to see
and like the night, too dark to see.
I ask myself, how long will I run?
How long do I resist friendship and fun?

Along comes another and another.
The walls are fastly cracking.
I try to repair, but I stand alone in despair.

Do I dare build these walls again, or do I accept
you as a true friend?

Jubee - Former Student

RISKING PROCESS

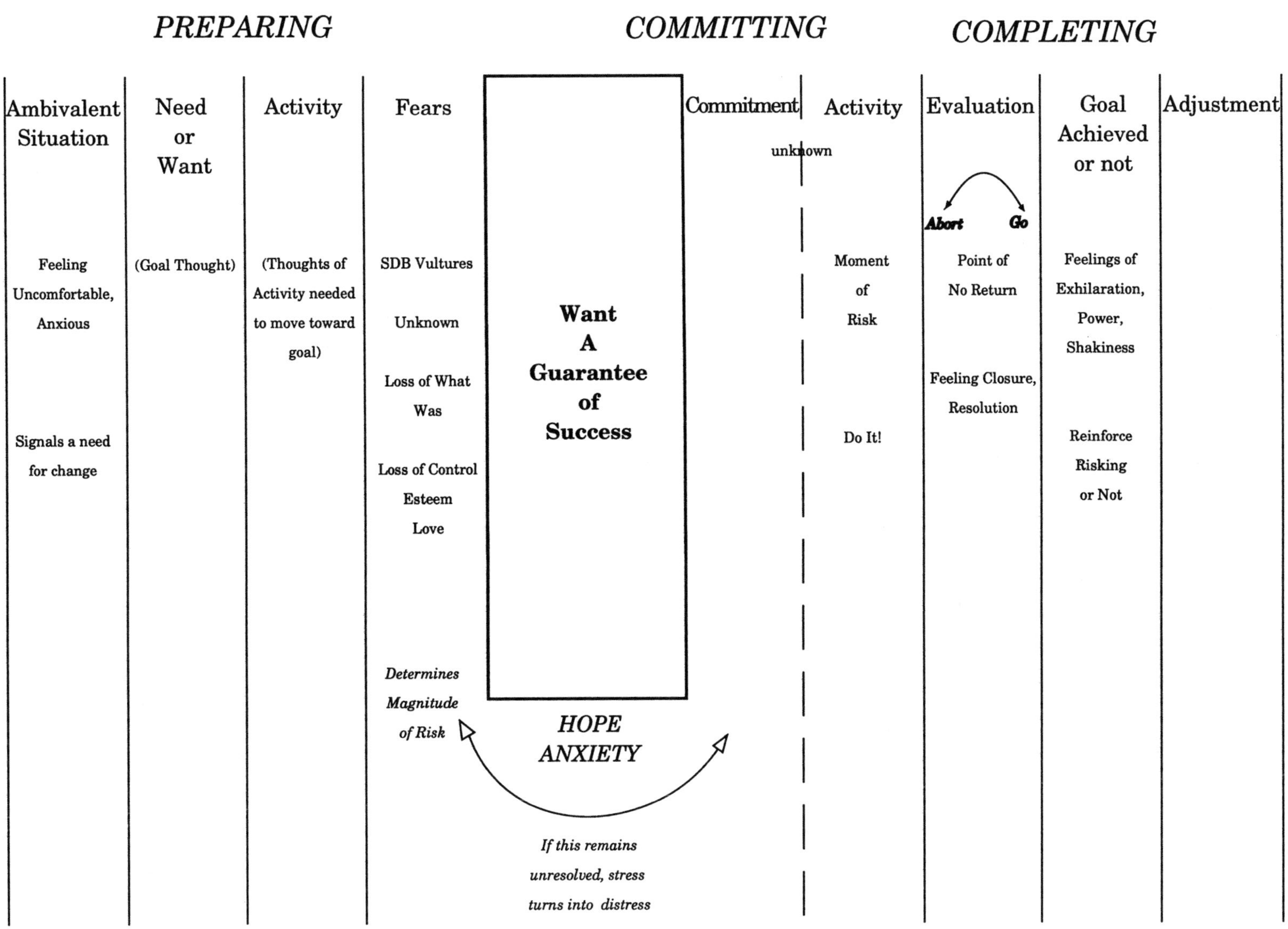

PREPARING   **COMMITTING**   **COMPLETING**

Ambivalent Situation	Need or Want	Activity	Fears	Commitment	Activity	Evaluation	Goal Achieved or not	Adjustment
Feeling Uncomfortable, Anxious	(Goal Thought)	(Thoughts of Activity needed to move toward goal)	SDB Vultures	unknown	Moment of Risk	Abort ↔ Go	Feelings of Exhilaration, Power, Shakiness	
			Unknown			Point of No Return		
Signals a need for change			Loss of What Was		Do It!	Feeling Closure, Resolution	Reinforce Risking or Not	
			Loss of Control					
			Esteem					
			Love					
			Determines Magnitude of Risk					

Box: **Want A Guarantee of Success**

HOPE
ANXIETY

If this remains unresolved, stress turns into distress

Figure 10

Chapter 7 - EPB Mind Stretchers

1. Describe the comfort myth?
2. What is the main idea of this chapter?
3. How are fear and hope related to risk-taking?
4. Draw and label the risking process chart and complete each stage by putting in an example of a risk your child has taken.
5. What might happen in the life of your daughter or son if she/he were to combine an enhanced self-concept with increased risk-taking? How far do you think they could go?
6. What are three important risks you think would enhance your child's life that they have been avoiding? What do you think about talking to them about these risks this semester?

SUCCESS TRIAD SUMMARY
Chapter 7 - Fear and Risk-Taking

CHALLENGES:

1. Understand the positive role of fear and discomfort as directionals for growth.
2. Be willing to experience discomfort in order to take the risks necessary for growth.
3. Differentiate between life enhancing risks and life limiting, restricting or potentially endangering risks.
4. Invest the necessary energy and patience to understand the nature of their fears and anxieties.

SUPPORT:

1. Provide the finances, equipment, or material necessary for your daughter or son to take life enhancing risks (ex. a computer for a journalism major, boots and sleeping bag for a backpacking trip).

CARING:

1. Encourage your son or daughter to take healthy risks for growth in spite of their perceived discomfort or fear.
2. Don't use threats and fear to intimidate, humiliate, or in any way denigrate your child in order to get them to take risks.
3. Let them know mistakes are expected when taking growth risks and it is OK to make them - they can learn from them.
4. Share your anxiety and fear about doing new things so they can see you actively involved in the risking process. This reinforces the fact that risking occurs throughout life whenever we wish to keep growing.
5. Encourage them to participate in activities that will contribute to their growth in spite of your own fears. Though difficult, work hard not to make your own fears and limitations those of your child.

106

NOTES

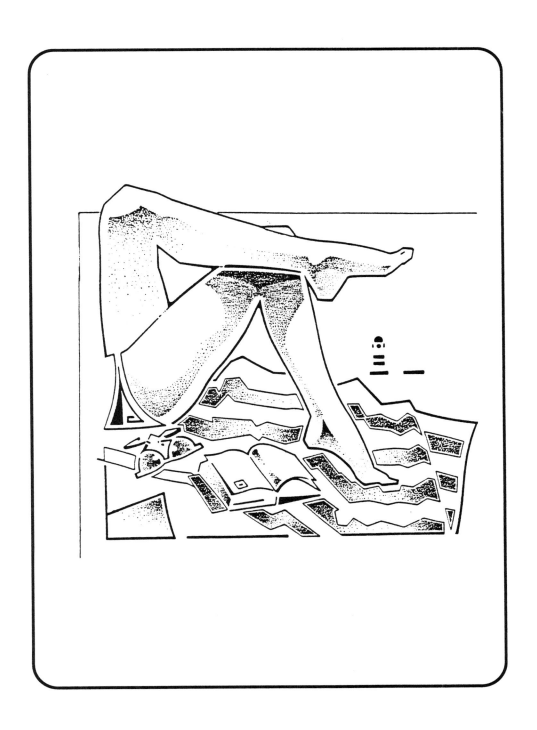

Chapter Eight
Sex-Role Stereotypes

WHAT IS SEX-ROLE STEREOTYPING?

One way of looking at sex-role stereotyping is that it is something that limits what both men and women can do to fulfill their potential. When the term 'sex-role stereotyping' is used, it frequently refers to the roles a man or woman is expected to follow in our society. Language, images, and attitudes all can convey sex-role stereotyping. Some examples of sex-role stereotyping by attitude are:

1. Men should not cry in front of others
2. Women should not worry about careers - after all, they are only waiting to find a husband.

The other terms used for prescribed roles are 'traditional' and 'non-traditional'. Traditional refers to that set of ideas about the functions of men and women which have been accepted and promoted by society in the past. Nontraditional means assigning roles to women that had been acceptable for men in the past, and assigning roles to men that had been acceptable for women.

Sex-role stereotyping can be learned in many ways. Often attitudes about the careers men and women are permitted to follow are learned through the family, mass media, school, or even history. For instance, learning about sex-role stereotyping begins at an early age. In children's storybooks, pictures and stories illustrate males playing the important or dominant role while females are taking minor roles.

While watching television, a child can learn that men's careers include doctors, lawyers, executives, and police officers. Women are generally shown as nurses, secretaries, or teachers. This gives children the idea that there are certain careers for men and certain careers for women.

In everyday language, sex-role stereotyping is apparent in the songs, commercials, and films we listen to and the newspapers and magazines we read. For example, the word 'housewife' is taken to mean that it is assumed that only females will be homemakers. 'Fireman' and 'repairman' indicate that only males do these jobs. The word 'girl' is used to describe women when the parallel word 'boy' would be considered inappropriate and insulting. 'Man' is still used to describe all human beings and its wide acceptance indicates how difficult it is to change perceptions; even ones that effectively leave out half the human race.

You may be thinking that things aren't as bad as they used to be; that they are changing. You are correct. We have seen fireman changed to firefighter and stewardess and steward to flight attendant and women move in greater numbers into positions of power and status. Now we even have a woman on the Supreme Court and have had a vice presidential candidate who is a woman. Yet sex-role stereotyping is still very much a part of our society; so much so that you will be confronted by it either subtly or overtly on a daily basis.

Looking at jobs with a nontraditional eye will help you to see that both males and females have interests and skills that allow them to do almost any type of work. Realizing this will enable you as a parent to be more sensitive to the choices your son or daughter makes. Listen to hear if they have examined all the options available to them instead of falling back on a stereotypic career because it is safer. It takes a self-confident student to go into a non-traditional field even today. So encourage your daughter or son to expand their possible choices of majors while in college so that future career choices are theirs based on their interests and abilities not on their gender.

In addition as you become more aware of sex-role stereotypes, you will notice that they impact the personal and social choices of your child as well as career choices. In keeping with the purpose of this book, it is hoped that you will support your child's efforts to expand her/his boundaries in all the life arenas based on choices she/he makes and not to settle for limitations to growth based on sex-role stereotypes.

Adapted from New Career Realizations
EVO Materials, 1979

Society's

Influence on

Sex Role

Developments

SOCIETY'S INFLUENCE ON SEX-ROLE DEVELOPMENT*

Before you go further in your thinking on the development of sex roles, please, complete the following rating scale. The scale measures the extent to which you think certain characteristics are true of you, your son, or daughter.

On the following page, you will find a large number of personality characteristics. Please use those characteristics to describe yourself. Indicate on a scale from 1 to 7, how true these various characteristics are of you. Please do not leave any characteristics unmarked.

Example: Sly

1	NEVER OR ALMOST NEVER TRUE that you are sly.
2	USUALLY NOT TRUE that you are sly.
3	SOMETIMES BUT INFREQUENTLY TRUE that you are sly.
4	OCCASIONALLY TRUE that you are sly.
5	OFTEN TRUE that you are sly.
6	USUALLY TRUE that you are sly.
7	ALWAYS OR ALMOST ALWAYS TRUE that you are sly.

Project BORN FREE
University of Minnesota

*Birk, J.M. Providing Life/Career Planning for Women and Girls.
National Consortium on Competency-Based Staff Development, in cooperation with
American Institutes for Research, Washington,1976.

Describe Yourself

1. Never or Almost Never True	2. Usually Not True	3. Sometimes but Infrequently True	4. Occasionally True	5. Often True	6. Usually True	7. Always or Almost Always True

_____ Self-reliant   _____ Reliable   _____ Warm

_____ Yielding   _____ Analytical   _____ Solemn

_____ Helpful   _____ Sympathetic   _____ Willing to take a stand

_____ Defends own beliefs   _____ Jealous   _____ Tender

_____ Cheerful   _____ Has leadership abilities   _____ Friendly

_____ Moody   _____ Sensitive to others needs   _____ Aggressive

_____ Independent   _____ Truthful   _____ Gullible

_____ Shy   _____ Willing to take risks   _____ Inefficient

_____ Conscientious   _____ Understanding   _____ Acts like a leader

_____ Athletic   _____ Secretive   _____ Childlike

_____ Affectionate   _____ Makes decisions easily   _____ Adaptable

_____ Theatrical   _____ Compassionate   _____ Individualistic

_____ Assertive   _____ Sincere   _____ Does not use harsh blanguage

_____ Flatterable   _____ Self-sufficient   _____ Unsystemic

_____ Happy   _____ Eager to soothe hurt feelings   _____ Competitive

_____ Strong personality   _____ Conceited   _____ Loves children

_____ Loyal   _____ Dominant   _____ Tactful

_____ Unpredictable   _____ Soft-spoken   _____ Ambitious

_____ Forceful   _____ Likeable   _____ Gentle

_____ Feminine   _____ Masculine   _____ Conventional

Directions for Scoring

1. Starting with the first descriptor, 'self-reliant', and continuing to the last 'conventional', mark each descriptor with either an 'M' (standing for masculine), an 'F' (standing for feminine) or an 'N' (standing for neutral). Continue marking all the descriptors, that is, M, F, N, M, F, N

2. For all adjectives that are masculine (that is, 'self-reliant' and every third adjective thereafter), add your ratings, then divide by 20 to get the average masculine score.

3. For the feminine adjectives (that is, 'yielding' and every third adjective thereafter), add your ratings, then divide by 20 to get the average feminine score.

4. Subtract the mean masculine score from the mean feminine score. The difference is your androgyny score.
    Feminine Score - Masculine Score = Androgyny.

5. Minus scores are representative of masculine-typed persons and plus scores are representative of feminine-typed persons. Scores within the range of -1 to +1 are representative of androgynous types.

ANDROGYNY - AN EXPLANATION

The rating scale you just completed and scored is the Bem Sex-Role Inventory (Bem, 1974). It is a measure of the construct, androgyny. By looking at ourselves in terms of how androgynous we are or are not, we are able to see the extent that our behaviors and personality characteristics are, according to society's stereotypes, either 'feminine' or 'masculine'.

What does it mean to be androgynous? If you are androgynous, then you are someone who has access to the full range of behavioral and emotional responses, and who freely can choose a response based on its appropriateness to the situation. An individual who is masculine-typed, is mainly characterized by traits which society has labeled 'masculine'. Such a person would find it difficult to display a 'feminine' trait, such as compassion, even when the situation would appropriately elicit compassion. Likewise, a person who is feminine-typed would find it difficult to demonstrate a 'masculine' trait, such as assertiveness, even when the situation would appropriately elicit that response. The androgynous person, on the other hand, is not typed one way or the other. The androgynous person possesses the full range of potential qualities, from masculine to feminine. Such a person can respond to a situation based on what is appropriate, and is not limited by one sex-typed set of characteristics or the other.

Society has not made it easy for individuals to develop a broad range of characteristics. On the contrary, if you are a woman, you have been reinforced for developing the 'feminine' characteristics. If you are a man, you have been reinforced throughout life for showing the 'masculine' traits. The advantages of being androgynous are clear:

1. If you are a woman, you are comfortable with your feminine identity; you possess such characteristics as tenderness, affection and nurturance, but you also possess and are able to demonstrate assertiveness, dominance, leadership, and other 'masculine' traits when the situation calls for them.

2. If you are a man, you are comfortable with being a man; you possess the characteristics that are socially reinforcing for men, such as leadership, competitiveness, and independence, but you are also comfortable with showing warmth, dependence, compassion, and other 'feminine' traits when the situation calls for them.

3. In relationship to careers, the individual who possesses a broad range of personality characteristics is most likely to consider a wide array of careers when faced with career decision making. Since the androgynous person isn't restricted to behaviors and roles traditional for his or her sex, career decisions would be made on the basis of interest, skills, values, and potential rather than on stereotypical expectations.

4.   This same principle applies to academic, social or personal decisions. In today's world women are called on to be wives, mothers, and income earners, and men are likewise being called on to be husbands, income earners, and fathers much more actively involved in the nurturing and raising of their children. This increasing role multiplicity is stressful and requires use of all our human potential if we are to handle the demands and opportunities with the flexibility needed for being successful. The person who is not restricted by sex-role stereotypes will decide based on his or her values, skills, attitudes, beliefs, and interests, knowing that in so doing they can bring all their potential into play when working to make their decision a reality.

Chapter 8 - EPB Mind Stretchers

1.   Define someone who is androgynous.
2.   How is sex-role stereotyping learned?
3.   How is sex-role stereotyping related to limited career and personal opportunities?
4.   What behaviors can you list that show you are sexist? Non-sexist? What sex-role behaviors did you teach your children that you think may limit their growth? Enhance their growth?
5.   What might happen in your personal relationships if you gave up several of your sexist behaviors? Your son's or daughter's relationships?
6.   What criteria would you use to assess someone's contribution to making this world a better place to live? Is one of your criterion sex? If so, why?

NOTES

SUCCESS TRIAD SUMMARY
Chapter 8 - Sex-Role Stereotyping

CHALLENGES:

1. Understand in what areas sex-role stereotypes have limited them.
2. Decide to develop their capabilities in areas that have been limited.
3. Be aware of how they may limit others based on sex-role stereotypes and commit to making changes toward fair and equal treatment.
4. Consider academic and career decisions based on interests, skills, and opportunities not on sex-limited stereotypes.

SUPPORT:

1. Fund your son's or daughter's participation in conferences or workshops which address the issue of sex-role stereotyping.

CARING:

1. Encourage your daughter or son to be all they can possibly be; consider all academic and career options without regard to sex-linked limitations.
2. Be aware of your own behaviors and attitudes that may be sex-role limited and commit to changing them. At least commit to not limiting your child's choices.

Chapter Nine
Relationships

RELATIONSHIPS

"There is no hope of joy except in human relations."
Saint-Exupery
(Flight to Arras, 1942)   Translated by Lewis Galantiere

Most college students would have little trouble agreeing with Saint-Exupery's quote. It seems that all kinds of relationships occupy an important priority in their lives from relationships with acquaintances, friends, best friends, parents, professors, staff, brothers, sisters, cousins, grandparents, dating partners, etc.

Though certainly joy can also be found in ways other than through human contact (ex. discovering the answer to a problem, seeing a beautiful rainbow, or playing with a kitten), it is difficult to imagine a person feeling joy who had no positive human relations. Understanding relationships and a willingness to put effort into making them more productive and enjoyable will enrich all arenas of your son's or daughter's life. A few of the important relationships that influence students while in college are addressed below.

Dating

It is the dating relationship or lack of one which is the central focus of many students' late evening talks, journal entries, worries, and hopes. This is natural as college provides an excellent opportunity for them to meet many interesting potential dating partners; some with similar interests, values, and life styles as well as differences that make them exciting. In the section, "Make Your Relationship Last," the dating relationship that becomes a primary love relationship will be addressed. The guidelines provided in this section will be helpful in all kinds of relationships if a commitment to following them is made.

A primary love relationship is not advisable for most first year students as it often severely limits individual growth opportunities. This statement may seem rather harsh to your son or daughter or even to you. I am not saying don't ever get involved in a primary love relationship. I am saying that most students miss a once-in-a-lifetime opportunity to learn more about themselves as well as others by dating a number of interesting people if they limit themselves to an exclusive relationship the first year. The development of deeper, more meaningful friendships is difficult once you become involved in an exclusive and restrictive dating relationship.

Dating can be a very enjoyable part of social life while in college. Open and honest communication between dating partners about the status of the relationship can reduce the unnecessary anxiety experienced by many students of not knowing where they stand. Communicating their level of interest in the other person, the nature of the interest (friend or

120

romantic), the time they wish to spend together, their likes and dislikes, whether the relationship is exclusive or open to dating other people, and the commitment to their dating partner will help alleviate the anxiety.

The two topics that students generally have the most difficulty with are whether their relationship is platonic or sexual and if sexual what are the parameters of sexual behavior and whether to have an exclusive relationship or one open to dating other people. If the relationship is open, students often fail to discuss whether the dating of others is to be platonic or potentially sexual. In today's world of AIDS, herpes, chlamydia, and numerous other sexually transmitted diseases, in addition to moral and ethical considerations, it is vital your daughter or son openly discuss these issues with her/his partner. The fact that such discussions may be uncomfortable and perhaps embarrassing is no excuse for not doing what is needed.

As parents more than ever before it is critical that you not fall back on simple moral, religious, or ethical positions and try to dictate sexual behavior to your child. It will not work and what is worse you are cutting your child off from a much needed source of support and love - yours. Learn as much as you can and make time to talk calmly and rationally to your daughter or son about their dating and sexual behavior. If you are too embarrassed to do this, please, encourage your child to talk to the available experts in the university health center, the counseling center, their physician, or public health official. Their life, the life of their dating partners, and their personal sense of self-worth and integrity are worth the risk on your part.

Friendships

Most dating relationships come and go, but friendships made in college often last a lifetime. These lifelong friends to be are people that your son or daughter as a first year student has just met or will be meeting. They will be a source of support, caring, challenge, sadness, happiness and any other emotion you can imagine. True friends don't agree on everything and can have heated debates over issues, academic or personal. Yet these disagreements tend to expand the boundaries of all concerned and therefore can contribute to the growth and strengthening of the friendship.

Balancing the demands of studies, personal time, dating, family, and friendships isn't easy. Friends should never be taken for granted, especially to devote attention to dating partners. When a person starts dating, of course, they must find time for this new person in their life. Too often students neglect friends and put most of their energy into the new 'love' interest only to find themselves isolated and alone when the love relationship ends. Someone worth dating will not ask your child to give up all of her/his time with friends just to be with him or her. As you talk with your daughter or son be aware of shifts in their relationships as they start new dating patterns. Encourage them to talk about the difficulty of balancing dating and friends plus school etc.

As parents most of us hope our children date and associate with persons who are decent, caring, and supportive of our child. This isn't always the case and parental intervention may be appropriate. Let me preface what I am about to say. Your child will and can do what she or he wants to do no matter what you say if that is their wish. If you have been working on open communications and demonstrating that you truly have your child's best interests at heart, you have a better chance of being listened to, understood, and seeing a change in behavior along the lines you are suggesting. So many times I have seen parents try to dictate to their children when they will date, whom they will date, etc. often with disastrous results for the child and parents.

I hope you will talk with your child and encourage them to develop relationships which contribute to their growth and that do not limit them. I would express deep concern if your child is involved in any relationship in which he/she is being hit or hitting their partner or in which verbal humiliation and intimidation are present. In such cases, ask your child how staying in such a relationship contributes to their growth. Let them know you see this relationship as limiting their growth and as being emotionally and perhaps physically harmful. Encourage them to seek counseling in the counseling center in order to understand what they really want in a relationship, how to get that, how to avoid pitfalls in relationships, and if necessary how to terminate an unhealthy relationship. Without a doubt students who have been in abusive relationships will tend to get into another abusive relationship unless they work through the issues that attract them to and keep them with people who are harmful to them. Counseling now while they are in college may save them much pain later in life and open them to new and positive aspects of themselves and relationships in general.

Professors

Though not friends in the way your child's peers are, college faculty can be a vital resource to them. Professors were not born with doctorates and a clear sense of what we wanted to become. Most of us had no clear career direction when we were undergraduates and few of us aspired to being college faculty when we were fresh out of high school.

Remember that we too were once first year students with hopes and aspirations and fears and self-doubts like those of your daughter or son. Over the years we've developed knowledge and skills and confidence by going through the same process of expanding boundaries as they are doing now. Some of us have worked hard to expand our boundaries and continue to work on our growth in many areas.

We went into teaching because we believe in young people and how important they are to the future of our country and our world. We also love learning and the joy of discovery. When we are good at our job your child can feel our excitement and commitment to our work and our caring and respect for them as growing young people. When we aren't good at our job, we can be uninspiring, negative, punitive, and disrespectful to them and their fellow students. When this happens I hope it is very temporary and that most of your child's contacts with us are positive.

Since they are a first year student, they may want to know how to address us. Many students have said they don't know whether to call us Mr., Mrs., Ms., Doctor, Associate Professor, Professor; very confusing compared to high school. Here are some helpful guidelines. Ask them to listen during the first class to how the faculty member introduces him or herself. Unless the professor says otherwise, they should address them the way they introduced themselves. If in doubt, use Professor before their last name. This is accurate for all of us and has the lowest possibility of offending anyone. Some of us can be very sensitive to forms of address.

Early in the semester it is advisable for your son or daughter to make an appointment with each of their professors. This is a time for them to introduce themselves, ask any questions about course structure, content, or requirements, and get to know a member of the faculty on a more personal level. At times they may feel that some of us are distant in class but most of us when approached out of class will appreciate their effort and enjoy the opportunity to meet them.

Also, your daughter or son should participate in class. Involved and inquisitive students leave good impressions and they will feel more comfortable, learn more, and enjoy class more. Talk with your child about these points and listen to hear what boundaries might stop them from following through on these suggestions. Encourage them to try them in spite of their discomfort and misgivings because of the potential for growth. This is an investment in their entire college career.

Parents

The relationship between parents and child is like no other relationship. It can be one of the most satisfying, loving, and rewarding or one of the most disappointing, uncaring, and fruitless relationships in your life and the life of your child. It is beyond the scope of this book to attempt to deal in depth with parent-child relationships. However, the guidelines below should help you to understand the nature of parent-child communications and to communicate in assertive ways that are healthy. The section in this chapter on conflict resolution provides concrete steps to take when the inevitable disagreements and conflicts arise.

Most students are aware that relationships with parents go through periods of good and bad times. Sometimes you may be aware that the responsibility for the difficulty or smoothness is more yours; at other times more your child's. Changes in the amount of freedom and responsibility they have and who is in control in the family often create unstable and unpleasant conditions.

Please remember that you are responsible for your communications, not your child's communications and they are not responsible for yours. You can hope they will change their way of communicating with you, but you are not in control of them. However, if you make a significant positive change in your communications with them, it is likely that they will respond positively over time.

For the longest period in their lives they have been totally or almost totally dependent on you, their parents. Appropriately they communicated to you as a child talking to a parent. Good parents provide nurturing, caring, and loving words as well as discipline when their child might be in danger or go beyond reasonable limits. Some parents are too often harsh, critical, and unloving with their words and inconsistent and severe in their punishment. In both instances these parents were in control and had almost total responsibility for their young child.

As your child got older ideally you would have given her/him more freedom as they were responsible enough to handle it. The communication was still heavily parent (in control and responsible) to child (not in control and not responsible) with times when your child may have suspected they were being treated more as an equal, an adult (relatively equal control and responsibility).

Now that they are in college, the freedom and responsibility they have has increased significantly. Realistically parents would find it difficult or impossible to control a college student's behavior and hopefully you wouldn't want to.

Along with your son's or daughter's increasing freedom and responsibility most parents recognize a decrease in their, the parent's, level of responsibility and control. For some parents it is very difficult to let go of the control; some think it would show you don't love your child or aren't interested in what's best for her/him. Unfortunately, this holding onto control is confusing two different things; *discussing with* your child and *dictating to* your child. Dictating is what you as parents did with small children. Now as a young adult they can discuss their concerns, hopes, etc. with you adult to adult.

Some of you have done well treating your child more as an adult as they grew older and were given more freedom and responsibility. Others of you haven't done as well and may find it frustrating to deal with your child as they find it frustrating to deal with you.

Students have complained that, "My parents are still trying to run my life even though they know I can do whatever I want!" "I've been home twice and they put a curfew on me like I had in high school! I felt humiliated and angry. They were treating me just like a child." True, the parents in these examples were trying to control their children. If students wish to deal effectively with parents who tend to treat them as children, it will require that they act as an adult, not a child. If the student in the example above slams the door to the house and doesn't come home until after curfew, he or she is acting as a child. An adult would express the belief that he or she is capable of setting a reasonable time to be home since they do it each day in college. The student may ask if there are concerns the parents have that they can talk over. Do you try to control your child's behavior? How do they respond when you do? Is this a growth enhancing arrangement for all concerned or a source of friction and unhappiness?

Often a non-defensive adult-to-adult approach can defuse a potentially volatile situation and open more productive lines of communication. Continuing with the example above, the adult-to-adult approach may have resulted in negotiating a mutually agreed upon time to be home or an agreement that no curfew was needed. If the parents still insisted on the same curfew, the student can express recognition of their right to set a curfew in their home and disappointment that they feel it is necessary. In this case the student would be looking at making changes in the curfew over several visits home. Of course the student may decide not to come home as often if the parents don't begin relating as adults to an adult.

As parents you can do a great deal to improve communications with your children but first be aware of the nature of your present communication and how it reflects your needs for control. Working toward greater equality and assertiveness will improve your relationship with your child and make an important contribution to your child developing the attitudes and behaviors necessary to be a successful and happy adult.

MAKE YOUR RELATIONSHIP LAST

As important as your daughter's or son's relationship is with you as parents, there is probably no other single activity in their lives into which they will invest so many of their hopes and dreams, as well as a great deal of their time and physical and emotional energies, as they will invest in their primary love relationship.

I believe we all want to be loved, to be that special person in someone else's life. It would be fantastic to be involved with someone with whom we can laugh or cry, be serious or silly, divulge our worst fears and greatest aspirations, have exciting and meaningful sex, and be respected, openly cared about and understood.

Such a dream can become a reality, but it isn't easy. With work and understanding of what makes relationships successful, couples can maneuver the pitfalls found in relationships.

Some sobering figures indicate the breadth and depth of relationship problems. The average relationship lasts three to four months; the national divorce rate is approaching 50 percent; the divorce rate for couples in which the man was 25 years old or younger at the time of marriage is closer to 85 percent; second marriages seem to dissolve at a rate comparable to first marriages, and spouse abuse occurs in one out of every three homes in the U.S.

Why do relationships get in trouble and eventually fail? What can we do to make our relationships more satisfying? Let's look at three major reasons and some solutions. Relationships fail: 1) out of ignorance of or an unwillingness to do what is required in a relationship, 2) from an over-emphasis on sex and confusion between sex, love, and intimacy, and 3) an exaggerated idea of personal risk for behaving in certain ways. Relationships require good communication, realistic expectations of our partner and ourselves in the relationship, and opportunities for both individuals to grow as human beings. They also require effort to put into action what is required.

Good communication is rare in relationships unless the couple has worked hard in this area. In our society, we are taught a language of disowning. We are taught to write in the third person, not to say, "I think this..." or "I feel that." This learning puts a boundary between ourselves and the people we want to get close to because the best way for that person to know what we think or feel is for us to tell them.

When we use "I" statements and are open in our communication, a sense of trust and understanding develops. Without a good communication base, the sharing of our joys, happiness, problems and frustrations is more difficult.

Unrealistic expectations are a major problem exacerbated by poor communication. If I expect you to be involved with me exclusively, and not have close male friends but don't tell you this, I have set up a covert expectation. If you expect me to make all decisions about where we go on dates and don't tell me, you have set up a covert expectation. Only expectations that are known to each other can be discussed openly. Too many hidden messages will almost certainly doom a relationship. Some other unrealistic expectations are that: 1) you must meet all my needs; 2) if you really loved me, you wouldn't show interest in other women/men; 3) I shouldn't get angry with you if I really love you; and 4) saying "yes" means "I love you" and saying "no" means "I don't love you".

Good relationships also require growth. Growth means change, and many of us don't want our partners to change; at least not in some of the ways they want to change. Out of our own feelings of inadequacy, self-doubt, sex-role limitations, or selfishness, we can behave in jealous, possessive and restrictive ways to prevent our partners from growing. We therefore prevent them from threatening our sense of comfort and security.

But this is truly one of the most tragic aspects of many relationships. *To love someone means a commitment to their growth and well-being as much as it is to our own.* Relationships without the growth of both partners are sure to come to an early demise or be filled with resentment and anger. A relationship committed to growth will be challenging as well as provide more opportunities for shared excitement and happiness.

In addition to ignorance of what is required in a relationship, an over-emphasis on sex is the second reason relationships fail. Intimacy and sex get confused and while we want both, we often get sex without intimacy. Intimacy is the degree to which we relate all we are to another human being without censoring our thoughts, feelings, or behaviors and the degree to which this individual reciprocates. Intimacy requires two people to communicate at a personally significant level.

Women, more frequently than men, believe love, intimacy and sex are very important in their relationships and that the three go together as one. Men more often than women have sex without much concern for love or intimacy. These perceptions of love, sex, and intimacy need to be communicated or they will become covert expectations, which can adversely affect a relationship.

The third major reason relationships get in trouble is our exaggerated idea of personal risk for saying what we think or feel or for behaving as we want. Most of us fear rejection. Rejection reinforces all the negative things we have ever thought about ourselves and contributes to our feeling less worthy. But if we are not willing to be ourselves, to go after what we want, to stand up for what we believe in, we have rejected ourselves. Such actions conclude that what your partner wants, thinks and believes is more important than what you want, think and believe. You give more worth to your partner than you do to yourself. Well, there is no one more worthy than you, nor less worthy. In a relationship, you can only give that which you have and are. Be the very best you can possibly be. It is ironic that the toughest thing in life is to be yourself.

Being yourself will require courage, openness, honesty and an assertive approach to life. Risks will need to be taken if you want to make meaningful changes in your relationships. Keep in mind that you will not be comfortable or secure when taking these risks. If you were, they wouldn't be true risks. Another way of looking at this is that growth only occurs when we risk expanding our boundaries into the unknown from the safety and security of the known, familiar and comfortable.

WHAT ENDS THE RELATIONSHIP?

One significant reason why relationships fail is that the perceptions we have of each other as men and women are faulty. It is our perceptions upon which we base our behaviors.

If you, as a male, perceive a female as weak, you will treat her as weak and expect her to act weakly. If you, as a female, perceive a male as insensitive, you will treat him as insensitive and expect him to act in an insensitive manner. When men or women do not behave as we expect, we are sometimes angry, sometimes pleased, more often confused. The perceptions we hold have a great impact on our relationships. (Review Chapter #8, Sex-Role Stereotyping)

To better understand these perceptions, students in a career development class were asked to respond to the following statement: "What would you do as a member of the other sex for 24 hours?"

Representative samples of their responses follow; they are organized in five categories: sex, social dating, body awareness, jobs and equality.

Sex   Both men and women were interested in experiencing life as a member of the other sex for a day. This interest was strongest for men.

Male:	"...flirt with every guy I saw...have sex with the first good looking guy I saw."
Female:	"Try to pick up a girl with a stupid line...have sex."
Male:	"I often wondered how a really good-looking girl looks at herself sexually and how she feels about sex. It seems that if a girl wants it, she can get it."
Female:	"I wouldn't walk by a total stranger and pinch her on the butt."
Female:	"I've always wanted to ask someone out or make the first move sexually because I never have."
Male:	"I'd go to the bar with some other cute girls, giggling, and ask for a drink. In an hour I'd have guys buying me drinks all night long."

Social Dating   Women had many more comments in the category of social dating than men did. Any man still entertaining the ideal that most women like the macho image might reconsider. Many of the men's comments in this category reflected anger and resentment over what they perceived as being used.

Female:	"First, I would try and act as human as I possibly could using human emotions that men try and hide. I would also stop the macho shit because it is incredibly boring to girls."
Female:	"Take my roommate dancing. She dates a macho jerk and should see what a nice, sensitive guy is like."
Male:	"I would get dressed up and go to the bar and have as many free drinks as I could get away with. I would hustle some guy into taking me to dinner and promise him a trip to the moon, then renege."
Female:	"I would date a lot of girls because it is socially acceptable for guys to date many girls even though it is frowned upon for girls to date more than one guy."
Male:	"Go to the bar and soak free drinks off of unaware guys."
Female:	"To start off, I am sick of hearing about sex from every guy I know. I would act like they do about it; talk rudely and say very forward things to people."

Body Awareness   Women also had more comments on body awareness than men. Both men and women embrace the fact that women are preoccupied with staying slim and that men do not share this concern.

Body image is a problem for many young women today.

Female: "Be able to eat massive amounts of food and run it off."
Male: "Realize I was getting fat so I would try and lose weight."
Male: "I'd look at myself in the mirror for a long time."
Female: "I would try to do all of the sports..."
Female: "It would be great just to have shorts on and not have to worry about hairy legs."

Jobs and Equality   The women were also more interested in jobs and the issue of equality.

Female: "I would apply for a job as a male, then later as myself, and see which got the job quicker-if either."
Female: "I would respect women's rights and not think of them as aggressive just because they want to be treated as equals."
Male: "I would get money (from husband) and go out and spend it (as women do)."
Female: "See if it's easier to get a job"
Female: "I would treat females better than what they are now treated."

A student, reviewing the comments wrote: "The majority of the replies from males seem to categorize females as mean, vicious and flighty. If they had a chance to be a girl, they would like to 'not pay' for a date, use female facilities, curl their hair, use make-up, and try sex from a female's point of view.

The majority of females said they would try corny one-liners that guys use in bars and see if they really worked, go around bare-chested, dress sloppily, be crude and obnoxious, and pinch girls' rear ends on the way to class."

In general, the students' perceptions reflect a lack of respect and trust between men and women. This lack of respect and trust can be a major factor interfering with good relationships. The comments also clearly show the power imbalance between men and women even though they didn't address this issue directly. The most telling sign of the imbalance was in their use of the words 'girl' and 'guy'. The parallel and power equal word for 'guy' is 'gal' and for 'girl' it is 'boy', yet you will not find one quote where 'boy' was used when 'girl' was used. This, along with references to all human beings as 'man' or 'mankind', is one of the most glaring and widely accepted forms of sexual discrimination in our country today. If you question the impact such language can have, address all men as boys whenever you would address women as girls and see what happens! Once again, your support of efforts on behalf of your daughter or son to grow in terms of equality and assertiveness will also contribute to her/him having healthier relationships.

Consider how many of the comments by their peers you find yourself agreeing with and think they would agree with. Try discussing your responses to the statement, "If I were a member of the other sex for 24 hours, I would..." with friends of the same and of the other sex, with your child, and especially with your partner if you are currently in a love relationship.

IMPROVING RELATIONSHIPS THRU CONFLICT RESOLUTION

One area that deserves special attention in improving relationships is conflict resolution. Conflict resolution is critical because it is the process by which problems or conflicts that can threaten a relationship are worked through; instead of greater misunderstanding and distance the result is greater understanding and intimacy between those involved. Good conflict resolution is difficult because it requires clear communication with ownership ('I' statements), openness, honesty, active listening, understanding of factual and emotional content, a willingness to admit being wrong, and a willingness to reach a mutually agreed upon resolution.

A most important rule in conflict resolution is to be assertive as opposed to aggressive or passive. Aggressive behavior where you violate others' rights to get what you want may produce the appearance of victory or agreement with your position, but this is seldom the case. Usually the other person feels threatened or intimidated and agrees in order to remove the threat. Also, once intimidation becomes a pattern, the other person is not likely to be as open and honest with you and the relationship begins to be deceptive and emotional distance sets in.

The person aggressed against in the above situation is acting passively or non-assertively; not standing up for his or her own rights and letting you violate his or her rights. They generally feel threatened and fear your rejection or other forms of emotional or physical harm. This person will feel much resentment and anger and though they don't often express it openly (except in occasional outbursts) they more subtly punish the aggressive party by lack of compliance.

Many relationships, if not most, characteristically have one person acting aggressively and the other passively; one person dominates and the other is submissive. Though such relationships may last a long time, they are filled with on-going fighting, making-up, distancing, lack of intimacy and foremost lack of love. To love is not to control another person and the only way adult relationships are true love relationships is when both partners act assertively the majority of the time.

To act assertively is to stand up for your own rights and at the same time respect the rights of your partner. This means equality of power where no one person dominates at the expense of the other. It means confronting your partner from a position of caring and love. It means showing as much interest in your partner's growth as in your own. It means being able to give and take. It means actively listening in order to understand your partner by putting your own needs on 'hold' until it is your turn to speak. It means working for a resolution of the conflict that if at all possible makes both of you winners. It means loving your partner. Do not expect to be able to do all these things at first. They take time, energy, commitment, and caring and are well worth the effort.

Below is an outline of points to keep in mind during a conflict:

I.   Prerequisite Understandings

      A.   Each person has equal rights and equal responsibilities.
      B.   If there is a conflict for one person, there is a conflict for both because the conflict affects the relationship.
      C.   Deal only with one issue at a time. Do not drag past conflicts and problems into the present situation.
      D.   Recognize your differences - not as good or bad; right or wrong. You are different people with different styles, different life experiences, and different perceptions of reality.
      E.   Conflict resolution is hard work and it takes time, commitment and effort.
      F.   Before a conflict erupts, agree with your partner on how you will handle it (see below).

II.   Communication Pattern

    A.   Time out. If you are so angry you cannot talk assertively, tell your partner how angry you are and that you will talk about this at a later time (set a time). Take some time out.

    B.   Do not try to push your anger aside. Go for a walk or do something physical to discharge some of the anger. Remember: ***DO NOT DO ANYTHING TO HURT YOURSELF OR ANYONE ELSE.***

    C.   Return at an agreed upon time to resolve the conflict. You may still be angry but now you should be able to express your anger assertively not aggressively.

    D.   Clearly state what you think the conflict or problem is, then actively listen as your partner does likewise. Listen to the words and the feelings that accompany them. Don't fall into the absolute trap. Words like always and *never* invite an argument over the absolute word itself instead of addressing the problem. Most couples have trouble agreeing to the problem. What chance do they then have of reaching an acceptable resolution?

    E.   Restate to each other what you thought you heard was your partner's idea of the problem. Clarify the problem until you agree what it is.

    F.   Each partner takes a turn offering solutions to the problem. Remember you are trying to get your needs met and so is your partner without violating each other's rights. This can be very difficult so both of you must be open to compromise, cooperation, accommodation or collaboration. There is no set rule that cooperating or accommodating is always best. For this reason, active listening to understand your partner and to understand yourself is crucial.

    G.   Check back with each other at a specified date to see how the agreement is working; modify if necessary. Be sure to recognize the effort your partner has made to change as well as areas that you still want changed.

    H.   Always remember that love can be hard work and that your greatest joys and closest intimacy often comes after such struggles to remove the boundaries between you.

Chapter 9 - EPB Mind Stretchers

1. What are the three reasons given for why relationships fail?
2. What is the main idea of the section on relating to professors?
3. Why is involvement in an exclusive primary love relationship not encouraged for first year students?
4. What are the features of a good relationship?
5. What would you predict would happen on your son's or daughter's next visit home if he/she acted like an adult when talking with you?
6. What are the most important qualities you hope your child is seeking in a best friend? Dating partner? Employer? Professor? Why are they similar or different? What are you looking for in them? What do you think they are looking for in you?

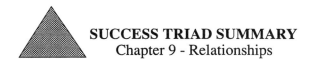 **SUCCESS TRIAD SUMMARY**
Chapter 9 - Relationships

CHALLENGES:

1. Develop relationships that are healthy because they contribute to the growth of the individuals involved and are open, honest, and supportive.
2. Differentiate relationships that are platonic friendships from sexual dating/love relationships.
3. Make decisions regarding their sexual behavior.
4. Take responsibility and ownership for communicating as an adult in their relationships.
5. Put energy into making healthy new relationships since their arrival at college has changed forever former high school relationships.
6. Increase the number and percentage of interactions that are assertive while minimizing those that are passive or aggressive.

SUPPORT:

1. Purchase resources(books) you believe will help them in relationships and with making decisions about their sexuality.

CARING:

1. Assess your relationship with your daughter or son and work toward a healthy balance of control and responsibility appropriate for a maturing adult.
2. Communicate with your son or daughter as one adult to another adult.
3. Be open and honest in your communications avoiding dictating to them. Practice true listening.
4. In your other relationships, especially with a spouse, work to model healthy communication and behavior patterns.

COMPONENTS OF ASSERTIVE, NON-ASSERTIVE, AND AGGRESSIVE BEHAVIOR

Although an outside observer cannot always tell if a person is expressing their emotions, exercising their rights or chosing situations in which to behave assertively, there are components of assertive behavior that are more observable. The following list will help you distinguish assertive, non-assertive and aggressive behavior.

Speech Characteristics

EVERYDAY BEHAVIOR	ASSERTIVE	NON-ASSERTIVE	AGGRESSIVE
LATENCY	Responds immediately. Does not interrupt, listens intently.	Long pauses before responding. Responses interrupted by hesitating.	Interrupts others, perhaps very abruptly.
VOLUME	"Normal" volume. Can be easily heard.	Voice very low. May be difficult to hear.	Speaks very loudly or may shout or yell.
INTONATION	Varies tone of voice to transmit feelings.	Voice very flat with no inflection. Monotone.	Tone may be strident and harsh.
DURATION	Varies- speaks until thoughts and feelings have been expressed.	Responses tend to be very short and sometimes incomplete.	Responses may be very lengthy and sometimes repetitious. May not allow others to have opportunities to speak.
BODY LANGUAGE			
EYE CONTACT	Makes frequent eye contact.	Seldom looks at others when speaking or being spoken to.	May stare or glare at others.
GESTURES	Hands are composed or used expressively.	May wring hands, clasp and unclasp fingers, fiddle with hair, jewelry or clothing, or make other repetitious movements.	May use gestures to intimidate: tap fingers impatiently, point or shake finger or fist.
POSTURE	Sits and stand straight and relaxed.	May be slumped or hunched over.	May be very rigid.

BODY LANGUAGE - CONTINUED

EVERYDAY BEHAVIOR	ASSERTIVE	NON-ASSERTIVE	AGGRESSIVE
FACIAL EXPRESSIONS	Expression reflects verbal content.	Expression may contradict verbal content, i.e., smiling when expressing anger or hurt.	May smirk or scowl.
DISTANCE	Maintains the normal appropriate, social distance. (1 1/2- 3 feet)	Greater distance is established. May move back.	Moves closer than normal distance.

VERBAL CONTENT

	ASSERTIVE	NON-ASSERTIVE	AGGRESSIVE
NON-COMPLIANCE	Refuses unreasonable requests or requests that conflict with own goals. Refuses politely, but firmly.	Usually complies with requests. May hint at desire to refuse.	Refuses abruptly and rudely.
REQUEST CHANGES	Explicitly requests specific changes in others behavior and mentions consequences, (positive, if possible), for making desired changes. May offer a compromise.	May vaguely imply that change in another's behavior is desired.	Demand change from others. Makes frequent use of negative consequences to enforce change. Refuses to compromise.
	Accomplishes refusals and requests for change by expression of own thoughts and feelings. Does not apologize for own thoughts and feelings and does not put self down. Supports statements when appropriate.	Frequently puts self down and apologizes for own thoughts and feelings.	Frequently attacks and labels others. Blames others. May resort to verbal abuse or swearing at others.

136

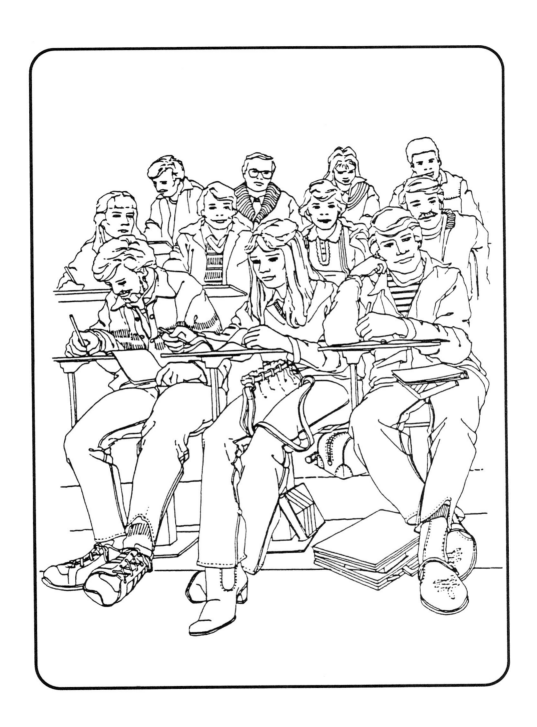

Chapter Ten
Learning Styles

LEARNING STYLES

Discovering how we learn is an intriguing problem that has received increasing attention in recent years. The discoveries in neuropsychology which have shed new light on brain functioning and research on effective learning styles have provided a vision of the learning process very different from that held a decade ago.

The research on the right and left brain functioning (actually the left hemisphere and the right hemisphere of the brain) demonstrates that each of us have a dominant hemisphere, one that we activate for most tasks. In the past, researchers believed the dominant hemisphere was the one responsible for language, the left hemisphere. We know now that in some people the language dominant hemisphere is the right. All of us use both hemispheres though we may use one more than the other.

It is important to realize that most classroom teaching appeals to the left hemisphere which is dominant in many people. This puts right hemisphere dominant people at a disadvantage in many classes. Below is a list of skills associated with the specialized skills for each hemisphere. Check those that you believe are strengths for your son or daughter.

Left Hemisphere

Handwriting
Symbols
Language
Reading
Phonics
Locating Details and Facts
Talking and Reciting
Following Directions
Listening
Auditory Association

Right Hemisphere

Spatial Relationships
Shapes and Patterns
Color Sensitivity
Singing and Music
Art Expression
Creativity
Visualization
Feelings and Emotions
Haptic Awareness

As you can see, the skills needed for success in traditional academic settings tend to be those involving the left hemisphere. Where are the strengths and limitations for your child? Are they similar to yours? Can you see how this may relate to your ease or difficulty in communicating with your child? Others?

I hope you will consider these as guidelines to understanding the basic specialization of the brain and realize that both hemispheres, to some extent, are often involved simultaneously in performing any of the above mentioned skills. Those students who are right hemisphere dominant will often have to work harder in traditional classes than those students who are left hemisphere dominant.

In addition to left and right brain, the related area of specific *learning styles preference* can have a major influence on your son's or daughter's ability to learn some academic subjects and therefore their emotional response to certain classes. The styles for our purposes correspond to the senses of hearing, smell, taste, sight, and touch (tactile). Remember that in the academic environment of most traditional classes the left hemisphere styles of hearing and sight dominate (lectures with notes on board) while the right hemisphere styles of smell, taste, and touch are secondary if they are used at all. Though your child will use all the various learning styles at different times and sometimes together, they will tend to favor one or two over the others.

In the classroom, the student with a primary learning style of listening will tend to like and learn more from a lecture than an equally gifted student who favors tactile involvement. Other students will say they need to see something in order to understand or remember it; these students' preferred style is visual. As you can quickly grasp, students who have a primary learning style of listening with a secondary style of visual will do fine in an academic environment which appeals heavily to both styles. Students with touch have restricted opportunities to use their preferred learning styles unless they major in hands-on fields such as engineering, art, music, etc. Those students (there are some) who learn best through taste or smell are virtually out of luck and must rely on their third or fourth preferred learning style in order to make it through college. Often these students have been turned off to learning in high school and never go to college.

If you think of the experiences your child has had with learning, in or out of school, you will be able to identify his/her learning styles. The exercise, Scale of Cognitive Style, which follows plus what you have recalled about your son's or daughter's childhood experiences with learning will help you to identify your child's dominant hemisphere and which learning styles they prefer. The benefits in knowing if your child is right or left hemisphere dominant, visual or tactile, etc. is in providing you the knowledge and understanding to assist them in making decisions to maximize their happiness and success in academic subjects as well as other areas of their lives. For example, if your child is right hemisphere dominant with a tactile learning style, lecture classes that are hearing and visual in style will not appeal to your child's strengths. For students going through the stress and adjustments that first term students experience, such a class can be difficult and or hard to concentrate in.

Your daughter or son can help her/himself in such a class by 'picturing' the lecture materials and taking notes, often notes that include pictures or diagrams which utilize the right hemisphere tactile learning style to some extent. In a more social context a woman (left hemisphere dominant and hearing learning style) will be more effective in understanding her right hemisphere dominant and visual male friend if she realizes he will perceive things differently than she will, that he will tend to convey the meaning of what he perceives based on his strengths and preferences, and that in order to truly understand each other she and he will need to be persistent and patient for neither one is necessarily more right or wrong. Think about your own family for a minute and the members that you relate easily to when explaining something and those with whom you have more difficulty. Is it possible that you are bringing different learning style preferences into play and could communicate more effectively if you understood each others strengths and weaknesses?

SCALE OF COGNITIVE STYLE

Circle the letter which best describes your son's or daughter's thinking, **A** or **B**. "My daughter (son) would say:"

1. I would rather work with mental puzzles and games.
   A

   I would rather work on real problems that people have.
   B

2. I start at the beginning to tell how something first happened.
   A

   I tell the most important thing and then the rest.
   B

3. I'm better at solving problems by breaking them down into parts.
   A

   I'm better at solving problems by thinking up different answers.
   B

4. I can always explain how I made a decision.
   A

   I can't always tell someone how I made a decision.
   B

5. I use my imagination when its necessary.
   A

   I use my imagination in most things I do.
   B

6. I can figure out what is going to happen next.
   A

   I can guess or sense what will happen next.
   B

7. I plan my work before I begin.
   A

   I plan my work as I do it.
   B

8. I look for the best way to solve a problem.
   A

   I look for different answers to solve problems.
   B

9. I finish one thought before changing the subject.
   A

   I often interrupt a thought to explain something else.
   B

10. My thinking is like words flowing through my head.
    A

    My thinking is like pictures flowing through my head.
    B

11. I always have questions about new ideas.
    A

    I agree with new ideas before other people do.
    B

12. I put each thing where it goes, after I use it.
    A

    I put everything away after I'm through with my job.
    B

13. I would like to be able to always control my feelings.
    A

    I would like to be able to be friends with everyone.
    B

14. Facts are more important than feelings.
    A

    Feelings are more important than facts.
    B

15. I'm good at making a plan and following it.
    A

    I decide what to do depending on the mood I'm in.
    B

16. When I work, I keep track of the time.
    A

    I don't think about the time when I work.
    B

17. Places don't change the way I feel.
    A

    Places I'm in change the way I feel.
    B

18. I can explain ideas so that others can understand them.
    A

    I can think of examples so others can understand the ideas.
    B

19. I do hard jobs first and then the easy ones.
    A

    I do the easy jobs first and save the hard ones for last.
    B

20. Sometimes I can't think of any answers to a question.
    A

    Sometimes I have too many answers to a question.
    B

21. I get my work done ahead of time.
    A

    I do my work at the last minute.

    B

22. The real me doesn't change much.
    A

    The real me is like many different persons.
    B

Total A's _____   **Total B's** _____

The totals indicate whether your son or daughter prefers a left brain (**A**) or right brain (**B**) style of learning. The greater the difference between the scores the stronger their preference. As you realize your son or daughter is not exclusively a left or right brain person; they well tend to be more right brain or left brain depending on a number of circumstances.

As your child grows, they hopefully will strengthen both orientations and be able to go back and forth between them based on which orientation would be most successful. For instance, a right brain approach would be more successful when creating the idea for a new song, while a left brain approach would be more successful in balancing a checkbook. Likewise, you will have greater success in supporting your son or daughter in college, if you are more right brained when trying to empathize with what they are feeling and more left brained when assisting them in filling-out financial aid forms. Review the material in the first part of this chapter and set some time aside to discuss it with you son or daughter in order for them to make the most of their preferred learning style.

ACADEMIC SKILLS

The outlines that follow are a reminder of key points for four academic skills areas related to your son or daughter being successful in college; test taking, note taking, research writing, and reading.

Review the outlines and see if you recall your child following the main points while in high school. If they did, good! You can check with them to see if they are currently using these ideas and if they aren't remind them of their effectiveness. If they didn't you may wish to review the outlines with them personally to see which points they are willing to adopt and again to encourage them to develop the discipline necessary to use these skills to be successful in their academic pursuits.

The Academic Skills Center in Moore Hall will provide workshops free of charge to assist in developing skills in any or all of these important areas. Encourage your child not to wait until she/he is in serious academic trouble to seek assistance. Remind them that a good student will utilize all the resources at her or his disposal. The Academic Skills Center is an excellent resource.

There are also many helpful books written on these topics. Check at your local bookstore, library, or the campus bookstore if you wish to do reading into any of these areas.

I would like to mention one special thought on test taking. From having taught or counseled thousands of students, I have found that a significant minority of them suffer from extreme test anxiety. Such anxiety is usually psychological in nature and is not remedied by using the test taking hints covered here or in other texts. If you are aware that your son or daughter suffers extreme anxiety encourage them to seek assistance from the University Counseling Center. Some symptoms of extreme anxiety are getting physically ill while studying for or taking tests, headaches or blurred vision while studying, sweating and rapid heartbeat, not being able to walk into the test site or leaving before finishing the test, going blank during the test, frequently forgetting material on the test and recalling it once the pressure of the test is over, verbal statements that their life will be ruined if they don't do well on the test, and obsessive talk or avoidance of talk about tests.

OUTLINE FOR TEST TAKING

1. Prerequisites for Successful Results:
    A. Be prepared
        1. Organize notes
        2. Annotate text
        3. Organize review schedule
        4. Complete all assignments
        5. Think positive
        6. Study with regularity

B.   Physical Conditions
1.   Sufficient sleep
2.   Don't alter physical self - state bound learning
3.   Comfortable temperature
4.   Eat lightly
5.   Comfortable seat and location
6.   Anxiety
    a.   Moderate amount - keeps you alert
    b.   Excessive amount - debilitating
    c.   Breathe deeply - use other relaxation techniques
7.   Equipment
    a.   Pens
    b.   Pencils
    c.   Erasers
    d.   Correction fluid - big assist on an essay exam
    e.   Calculators - other specialized equipment like computer discs

C.   General Principles
1.   Survey and plan time wisely - save time to review answers
2.   ***READ ALL DIRECTIONS CAREFULLY***
3.   Understand terminology
4.   Answer easiest questions first
5.   Attempt every question
6.   Actively reason through questions
7.   Changing answers
    a.   Generally not a good idea - go with initial reaction
    b.   Change if you can see a rationale

II.   Types of Tests:
A.   Objective

1.	True - False	Requires
2.	Multiple Choice	Recognition
3.	Matching	
4.	Completion	Requires Recall

B.   Essay
1.   Short answer
2.   Lengthy
3.   Determine correct terminology - describe, analyze, compare, contrast, etc.
4.   Survey and plan time

5.   Jot notes for each question

      a.   Organize answer by outlining notes
      b.   Reduces likelihood of forgetting to include material
6.   Write
7.   Proofread answers
8.   Use test results
      a.   As a study guide
      b.   As an indication of how you rank
      c.   Point of reference if you question results

OUTLINE FOR NOTE TAKING AND RESEARCH WRITING

I. Note Taking
  A. Rationale
     1. To organize and reduce material in order to learn and remember
     2. Students who study their notes, using recitation, have 11/2 times greater retention after six weeks than those who do not
     3. Those who take no notes forget 80 percent by the end of two weeks

  B. Five - Step Process
     1. Record
     2. Reduce
     3. Recite
     4. Reflect
     5. Review
  C. Methods
     1. Note paper
     2. Note cards
     3. Cornell System
  D. Positive Attitude
     1. Anticipate by reading material
     2. Take key ideas
  E. Listening vs Hearing
     1. Listen - absorption
     2. Take key ideas
  F. Review Notes
     1. Immediacy - within 24 hours
     2. Frequency - daily and weekly schedule
     3. Hint: use your computer - put questions on disc with answers in 'hide type' for review

Cornell System

```
+----------+--------------------------+
|          |                          |
| R        |                          |
| e        |                          |
| d        |        Record            | 9"
| u        |                          |
| c        |                          |
| e        |                          |
|          |                          |
| 2"       |        6"                |
+----------+--------------------------+
|          Reflect            2"      |
+-------------------------------------+
```

II. Research Writing
  A. Choosing Topic
     1. Narrowing scope
     2. Being inclusive enough
  B. Researching
     1. Note cards vs sheets of paper
     2. Bibliography cards
     3. Put on computer disc
  C. Outline
     1. Sets pattern of approach to writing
     2. Can be organized from note cards

D.   Writing the Paper
1.   Use your computer and an appropriate word processing program with spell check
2.   Rough draft
3.   Set aside to gain distance and perspective
4.   Revise and polish
5.   Finished product (have you run spell check!)

OUTLINE FOR EFFECTIVE READING

I.   Reading Effectiveness

    A.   Rationale
        1.   Too many students cannot read critically and cogently.
        2.   Cannot make connection between author's message and something in their own mind.

    B.   Requirements
        1.   Disciplined, purposive research
        2.   Critical spirit - healthy skepticism and curiosity

    C.   Reading is a thinking process entailing an ability to:
        1.   Remember
        2.   Understand
        3.   Interpret
        4.   React to and evaluate

    D.   Speed and comprehension - increase in rate has been paralleled to increase in comprehension.
        1.   Desire to improve
        2.   Willingness to try new techniques
        3.   Motivation to practice
            a.   Eye-span exercises
            b.   Timed-reading drills

    E.   Skimming - searching for main idea through first and last paragraph, topic headings and organizational cues.

    F.   Scanning - running your eyes down the page looking for specific facts or key words or phrases.

    G.   Vocabulary Building
        1.   Underline new words and write definitions in the margin
        2.   Write words and definitions in cover of texts listing page number as well as for a cumulative glossary
        3.   Read, read, read
        4.   Incorporate new words into your vocabulary

    H.   Listening - reinforces critical thinking
        1.   Radio interviews and commentaries

    2.   Television interviews and commentaries
        a.   Purposive attitude
        b.   Open and objective mind
            1.   No preconceived attitudes
            2.   Postpone evaluations until end of presentation

I.   SQ3R
    1.   SURVEY - read chapter's title, first paragraph headings and last paragraphs
    2.   QUESTION - connect headings into questions - gives direction to reading
    3.   READ - by section trying to identify main points and relating to previous sections
    4.   RECITE - immediately after reading each section, try to recite what you have read adjusting length of recitation to approximately one page at a time
    5.   REVIEW - review entire selection subsequent to completing all sections using the reading and reciting phases.

II.   Concentration - elusive, only happens when we don't think about it.
    A.   Difficulties in concentration
        1.   Fear of failure
        2.   External distractions - planes, trains, friends, telephone calls, TV, noise
        3.   Internal distractions - daydreaming, personal problems, indecision, mental fatigue, loneliness, physical fatigue

    B.   Aids to help in concentration
        1.   Positive attitude
        2.   Particular place for study
        3.   Equipment assembled
        4.   Good lighting and comfort
        5.   Eliminating distractors
        6.   Established goal for study session

III.   Memory
    A.   Types of memory
        1.   Sensory
        2.   Short-term
        3.   Long-term

    B.   Methods of Remembering
        1.   Recall - being able to give back items or ideas

2. Recognize - being able to pick out original items from a list or statement
3. Relearning - relearning a second time, will be easier to do than originally
4. Recitation - key to remembering, putting the author's words into your own for encoding and relating to already known concepts
5. Memorizing - not as much value as reciting, much too remote
6. Mnemonic Devices - means 'to help memory' Ancient Greeks devised them for oration
   a. Acronyms - first letter of each word to form a word
      1. HOMES - Huron, Ontario, Michigan, Erie, Superior
      2. ROYGBIV - red, orange, yellow, green, blue, indigo, violet
      3. SPA - Socrates taught Plato, taught Aristotle
   b. Rhymes
      1. 30 days has September, April, June, and November. All the rest have 31, except February, etc.
      2. I before e except after c
      3. Principal is a pal, principle is a rule
   c. Association
      1. Tropic of Capricorn is in the Southern Hemisphere, you associate corns with your feet which is your south
      2. Longitude and latitude - associate the N in longitude with the N of North to remember the lines of longitude run north and south
C. Mapping - 'picturing' the material, pictures, charts, and graphs
D. Pegging - recalling a peg word to which you hook the word or term, example - one bun, two shoe, three tree, etc.

Chapter 10 - EPB Mind Stretchers

1.   What are two skills which your daughter or son possess associated with the left hemisphere of the brain?
2.   What is the main idea of the section on learning style preferences?
3.   Why is knowing your son's or daughter's preferred learning style significant?
4.   What two preferred learning styles have the advantage in most academic classrooms?
5.   How would you encourage your child to create a classroom environment that appealed to his/her preferred learning style? What would you encourage them to do in classes that appeal more to their learning style weakness?
6.   What do you think about the relationship between your preferred learning style and that of your child (spouse, employer, other children, employees, siblings) and your ability to communicate and understand each other? How can knowing your preferred learning styles make communication more effective?

SUCCESS TRIAD SUMMARY
Chapter 10 - Learning Styles

CHALLENGES:

1. To determine whether they are right or left hemisphere dominant and their preferred learning style and to use this knowledge to help shape learning environments to meet their potential.
2. To not look at their or another student's style as 'good' or 'bad', but as different and having both its strengths and limitations depending on the circumstances.
3. To talk to a learning specialist if they encounter a marked drop in their academic performance not accounted for by purely social or personal concerns.

SUPPORT:

1. Provide the funds necessary to pay for special testing by a learning specialist if your child suffers a marked drop in academic performance not accounted for by purely social or personal concerns.

CARING:

1. Encourage them to do whatever amount of work they need to do in order to be successful (and not neglect a balanced personal and social life) recognizing that some of their friends won't need to work as hard and others may have to work harder.
2. Encourage them to utilize their preferred learning styles whenever possible and to strengthen their non-preferred styles when needed.
3. Encourage them, as needed, to take advantage of the free workshops on reading, writing, test taking, and note taking offered by the Academic Skills Center in Moore Hall.

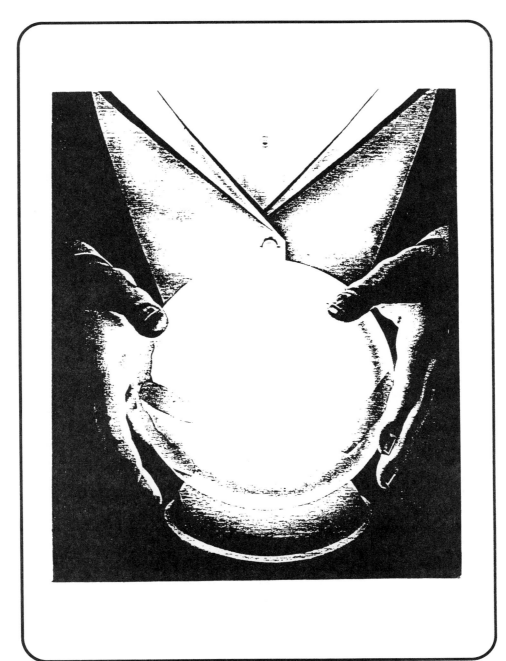

Chapter Eleven
Decision Making

DECISION MAKING

Your children make decisions every day - hundreds of decisions. Some decisions are made so quickly they might not even be aware they made a decision while other decisions have been thought out carefully and perhaps even agonized or rejoiced over. Yet some people are better decision makers than others. By better I mean they are willing to make more decisions to get what they want in life and their decisions result in them succeeding more often than people who are not good decision makers. What makes a good decision maker?

Good decision makers have an excellent working knowledge of their circumstances, themselves and the stages of the decision making process. Let's look at each of these major areas in some detail.

In order to have an excellent working knowledge of themselves, your daughter or son would be aware of her/his values, beliefs, attitudes, how they feel about themselves, and how they feel about how others perceive them. As you have read through this book you have done considerable thinking and work on values, beliefs, and attitudes which, as you have shared this with your college age child, can aid him/her in becoming a better decision maker. In addition, if they are feeling in control of their lives (at least what they can control), like themselves, and are sensitive to others without putting their own needs aside, they will tend to feel confident enough to take responsibility for the consequences of the decisions they will make. Often people who do not like themselves, feel someone or something else controls most of their lives and look for others' approval at the expense of their own growth needs will not feel confident enough to take responsibility for their decisions.

For these reasons self-responsibility, self-understanding, and understanding the importance of risk-taking to meet your needs and wants and to increase your sense of competence and control have been emphasized. This has been put in the context of acting assertively which makes your son or daughter sensitive to others' rights as well as her/his own and the concept of social and environmental responsibility which recognizes their responsibility to contribute positively to the people and planet of which they are a member.

With such a solid understanding of themselves, they can be a powerful decision maker if they understand and utilize the process of decision making. Since it is a process it has the potential to be very simple (decision to brush teeth) or very complex (decision to disarm nuclear devices) depending on the above mentioned knowledge of the individual or individuals involved and the 'facts' found in the world outside the individual. As you can see, the more people involved in a decision the more complicated it is potentially. The following stages are useful to review with your child when they are confronted with decisions that are for them more complex:

Stage 1 - *Problem Identification* - often past over by many people in the rush to alleviate anxiety or gain excitement by taking action. Clearly define what your problem is before proceeding.

Stage 2 - *Generate Alternatives* - there is always more than one answer to a problem; be creative and generate as many possibilities as you can without worrying how 'crazy' some may seem.

Stage 3 - *Choose Among Alternatives* - narrow your list to 3-5 alternatives you think are worthy.

Stage 4 - *List the Consequences of Each Alternative* - what happens if each alternative is carried out? Recognize that though you can determine much of what might happen it is very unlikely, especially on complex decisions, that you will cover all the consequences.

Stage 5 - *Choose A Goal* - decide which alternative gives you the *best* chance of achieving the *optimal* solution to the problem.

Stage 6 - *Develop A Plan to Accomplish Your Chosen Alternative* (now called goal) - what are all the steps, people, resources, time, etc. needed to accomplish your goal. There are *no perfect plans* that *guarantee* 100% success with no *risk* of negative consequences. Your plan should reflect a synthesis of what you know about yourself, others, your resources, and your problem.

Stage 7 - *Implement Your Plan* - this is the riskiest part for most. The time to fully commit and take action. Don't let the first feelings of discomfort cause you to abandon your plan. Give it a reasonable chance to succeed by believing in it and committing your energy and resources to accomplish it.

Stage 8 - *Evaluate the Progress of Your Plan* - adjust when and where needed to keep your plan on the target of achieving your goal.

Stage 9 - *Goal Achieved and Problem Solved or Not* - if yes, celebrate and adjust based on your success. If not, recheck the problem and start the process again.

Any decision your son or daughter makes can be run through this process, but for most decisions this would be an incredible waste of time and it would effectively immobilize them from taking action on many things they now take for granted. Imagine using, at a conscious level, this process to decide things like tooth brushing, hair combing, eye winking, saying hello, writing each letter in the alphabet, speaking every word, rubbing your nose, looking at a tree and on and on!

Your child is truly an amazing decision maker. If you want them to be good at the tough, complex decisions though, the process outlined above will be an extremely helpful guide. I think you can see how successful completion of the appropriate tasks outlined by Chickering and Perry result in a young adult more prepared to accept responsibility and feel confident and competent enough to make the important decisions they need to make while in college. As usual this takes discipline, effort and commitment on their part and yours. But you are used to that by now!

CONSENSUS DECISION MAKING

Once you start observing the decision making process that takes place in the groups you belong to, you will see that individuals can reach a decision for themselves only to find out the other members of the group have reached a different decision. Then the group must reach a decision through use of one of several possible approaches.

One approach is the democratic strategy; one person, one vote. Though this approach is supposed to reflect a collective judgment because people were involved in the decision, it often doesn't. Another approach is the dictatorial strategy where one person has the power to 'force' compliance with his or her decisions whether others agree or not. A related strategy is the 'charismatic leader' method, where one individual is so personally powerful and attractive to group members that they will often go along with the leader without objection or serious consideration of the problem. Think over your past experiences in group decision making and you will quickly identify several different approaches. What strategy was used in your family, classes, first job, and peer group when you were growing up? What strategy do you use with your spouse and children now?

There is a strategy of decision making that truly involves all persons responsible for a decision. The consensus strategy means that all persons involved have reached substantial agreement, not necessarily unanimity. The important advantage with the consensus strategy is that the goal is reached through group effort, all persons are asked to give their input, few assumptions are made, there are no large pockets of minority resistance that were 'voted' down to deal with, and everyone has ownership for the decision and commitment to its solution.

Hidden Agendas

Each group member brings her/his own individual motivations to any group decisions. They have an understanding of the task or problem facing the group and they come to the task with needs of their own. These are personal needs and motives and often involve issues of acceptance, status, power, self-worth, belonging, recognition, control, and productivity. Such needs are natural and can add to an individual's commitment and effort in the group. However, if an individual's needs conflict with another's needs or the progress of the group toward its goal, then an impasse occurs that must be addressed if the group is to be successful. The process of addressing this impasse is called confrontation. Confrontation keeps disagreements out in the open where they can be dealt with instead of forcing them underground as hidden agendas which can disrupt goal setting and decision making from corporate boardrooms to family meetings. In the consensus strategy, individuals do not try 'to win' for themselves at other's expense. They try to reach a group decision that reflects commitment in varying degrees for all members; in this way everyone wins.

Suggestions for Consensus Seeking

Consensus seeking by a group can be time consuming and hard work. The reward for such effort can be a well-functioning, successful group with high morale because all members are actively involved and working together for the benefit of the group. The following guidelines will be helpful in your efforts at reaching group consensus:

1. Members should not try to 'win' as individuals. Listen to other members and try to reach a collective agreement so all individuals 'win' and the group 'wins'.
2. Conflict should be viewed as potentially helpful. Avoid changing your mind in order to reach agreement and avoid conflict. Support solutions with which you are able to agree, somewhat, at least.
3. Members should actively listen to and be listened to by group members.
4. Tension-reducing behaviors are okay, so long as conflict is not smoothed over prematurely thus masking true resistance.
5. When the work is becoming ineffective individual conflicts and the decision-making process of the group should be discussed.
6. The most creative and satisfying results flow from a fusion of information, logic and emotion. (Pfeiffer and Jones, 1973)

Chapter 11 - EPB Mind Stretchers

1. What method of decision making provides for more group involvement and a greater sense of ownership in the eventual decision; the democratic or consensus method?
2. What is the main idea of the section on Hidden Agendas? What hidden agendas do you take into talks with your college age daughter or son?
3. How is the decision-making process related to the risking process studied in Chapter 7?
4. Select a problem that you have not yet reached a decision about. Following the nine stage decision making process, write down all the information you can at this time. Come back to the process until the decision has been implemented and the process completed.
5. What might happen if you were to combine your knowledge of consensus decision making and relating to children (Chapter 9) the next time your family had a problem to solve?
6. What aspect of the consensus decision making process do you think would be most difficult or uncomfortable for your child? How will you support them in overcoming this barrier?

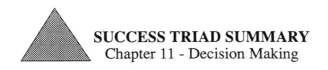

SUCCESS TRIAD SUMMARY
Chapter 11 - Decision Making

CHALLENGES:

1. Accept responsibility for the consequences of their decisions.
2. Become aware of their own needs and sensitive to others; to act assertively.
3. Possess enough self-love to commit the energy required to understand themselves, their circumstances, their resources, and their goals and to implement the necessary actions to reach their goals.
4. Accept success and the responsibilities that go with success.
5. Accept failure and the responsibilities that go with failure.
6. Differentiate between 'important' life decisions which require considerable thought, research, and implementation time and 'less important' decisions.
7. Accept that some goals don't have immediate short-term rewards yet are worth the discipline and effort it takes to reach them.

SUPPORT:

1. There may be a time when the consequences to your daughter or son for a decision they made would inflict more long-term harm than good. If you realize that the lesson has been learned and there is no real benefit to your child to suffer such harsh consequences, you may offer whatever monetary or material resources you think are justified and bring the incident to closure. *Caution:* This is one of the most difficult decisions for a parent and only rarely is it advisable to intervene in the process of your child taking the consequences for his/her decisions.

CARING:

1. Believe in them and their abilities and encourage them to make decisions on their own-to take life enhancing risks.
2. Empathize with them when they fail and help them to learn from their failures.
3. Help them to accept that the consequences for their decisions are theirs, not yours or anyone elses.
4. Occasionally ask how they are progressing on long-term goals. Let them know you understand the discipline required to postpone the more immediate gratification of short-term goals. Encourage them to persist.
5. Celebrate their successes with them! Show your pride in them.

CONSENSUS - SEEKING BEHAVIOR RATING SCALE

Circle the number that, in your judgement, represents the way members on your team behave. Write the reason for your scoring in the section labeled "Comments". When you have finished, discuss the scores together, come to a group judgement about the appropriate number.

	Hardly any of us ever do this.	Once in a while we do this.	About half the time we do this.	We do this most of the time.	This is a real strength of our team.
Express Ideas Freely	1	2	3	4	5
COMMENT:					
Express Feelings Openly	1	2	3	4	5
COMMENT:					
Listen to Others	1	2	3	4	5
COMMENT:					
Look for Similiarities in Differing Points of View	1	2	3	4	5
COMMENT:					
Honor Comments of All Team Members	1	2	3	4	5
COMMENTS:					
Work Together as a Team	1	2	3	4	5
COMMENT:					
Work Toward Team Goals Rather than Individual Goals	1	2	3	4	5
COMMENTS:					

Chapter Twelve
Tolerance, Acceptance and Sociometry

TOLERANCE AND ACCEPTANCE

Have you wondered if your child is really growing, really learning, or really getting everything out of their experience so far? They are nearing the end of their first semester in college. From years of working with students, I have found many, perhaps most, students have great difficulty seeing or assessing in any concrete way their growth and learning. The goal you will remember was to provide you the information and process necessary to support the efforts of your college age daughter or son to expand his/her perceptual boundaries in various arenas in order for them to be happy and successful. Two concepts that capture the growth implicit in this goal are the concepts of tolerance and acceptance. What do these have to do with growth, success and happiness in life much less academic success? Everything!

Think of it this way: the breadth and depth of your child's happiness and success is directly correlated with their degrees of tolerance and acceptance. Before we pursue this further, acceptance is the act or process of receiving gladly or taking willingly; tolerance is the capacity for or practice of allowing or respecting the nature, beliefs, or behavior of others.(American Heritage Dictionary, 1976) Getting back to how these concepts correlate with happiness and success, think of your son being in a class where he was intolerant of the ideas presented and certainly wouldn't accept them. How happy and successful is he likely to be in such a course compared to a class where at first he is tolerant of ideas he doesn't accept and then accepting of some of them after study and consideration?

Apply this to personal relationships and the impact can be dramatic. If your daughter believes in personal freedom with responsibility (right to vote, free speech for example) how happy and successful would she be in a totalitarian society that was intolerant and unaccepting of her beliefs and behaviors? On the other end of the continuum, how happy and successful would she be in a relationship with someone who accepts her for who she is and even tolerates some of her most maddening behaviors? Mahatma Gandhi had enormous boundaries of tolerance and acceptance and as a result had many people who liked, loved, and cared about him all over the world and many people that he could like, love, and care about also. Many of you are familiar with Dr. Leo Buscaglia, the 'Love Doctor', who has become famous for writing, lecturing, and communicating any way he can about being a loving person; about expanding your tolerance and acceptance boundaries of yourself, others, and your world.

People with narrow tolerance boundaries like Hitler, Mussolini, and religious, social, and political fanatics have few people they can give to or receive from liking, caring, and loving. And since they are constantly coming into contact (boundaries collide) with people who do not fit into their tolerance and acceptance boundaries, they often are angry, stressed, upset, and unhappy.

Have you ever thought about the world's problems in terms of tolerance and acceptance? Why is there so little peace and so much war? Why do we have trouble coexisting with the Soviets? Why is there so much religious persecution and racial bigotry? Why as a species do we show so little respect for our planet and the life on it? Why is there so much strife and conflict in our families? And most sadly why is there such widespread verbal and physical abuse of our children; our most beloved and precious resource?

Tolerance and acceptance are worthy goals for all human beings. The more tolerant and accepting your children learn to be, the greater their chances of being happy and successful in an increasingly stressful yet still infinitely beautiful world. As you prepare to welcome home your son or daughter for the holidays, think back on their childhood at home, school, religious affiliation, etc., in terms of tolerance and acceptance. When home use the tool of sociometry which is explained below to better understand them, your family and friends. Then I hope you will choose to expand your tolerance and acceptance boundaries. It can go a long way toward making you a happier and more successful person, a more supportive and caring parent, and it might just contribute to making this world a nicer place to live.

SOCIOMETRY

Sociometry, the study of individuals interacting as part of a group, can be a useful method to apply when viewing family interactions. Thanksgiving and the Holiday Season gives you an opportunity to view your family from a new and different perspective. Having been away at college for some months, your daughter or son is in a better position to see family interactions more clearly and accurately. Sometimes this is very disturbing to them as they can see more clearly that which is unhealthy and limits their opportunities for growth. Sometimes this is very positive as they see strengths of the family as a unit and individual family members that they hadn't seen or appreciated before. Having progressed this far in this book, you too, are aware of family dynamics, yours and others, which could be changed and attitudes and behaviors which could be added to make your family members happier and more successful. Though it can be uncomfortable and difficult, you may wish to hold individual or a family discussion about making changes to improve the family environment so all members begin to feel more support, caring, belief in them, and love. Once each person has decided on a change he/she can make they commit to putting the effort necessary into accomplishing this change and you agree on a time to sit down again and assess the progress made as individuals and as a family. From this people are reinforced for successful changes and encouraged to continue their growth.

You can use much of what you have learned in the previous chapters more effectively when you understand the sociometry of your family. You will be able to assess situations and act in your best interest when the communication and power lines are clear and the role of each family member is spelled out.

Figure 11
Sociogram

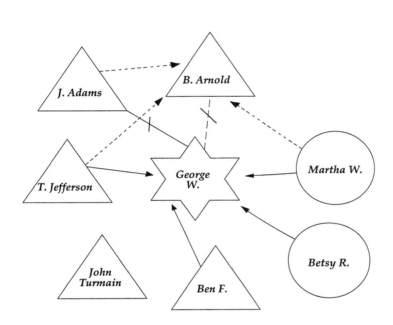

Locate:

the sociometric star
the rejectee
the isolate
the isolated diad

One way choice	⟶
Reciprocal choice	——
One way rejection	– – – –▶
Reciprocal rejection	— — — —

NOTES

A Sociogram is a diagram of the interactions between people. It is a statement of the moment and will change with both time and criteria.

In the sociogram depicted, the criterion might have been, "Who would you most like to see run our country?" If the criterion was, "Who would you most like to dine with this evening?" the sociogram would be very different. Selecting the correct criterion is vital. If you want to know who a person would like to work with, don't ask who they would like for friends.

Individuals select different people on the basis of criteria. One can take advantage of this when integrating an isolate or rejectee into a group. If the criterion for the above sociogram was, "If you were lost in the wilderness, who would you most like to be with?" Lewis and Clark would quickly be integrated into the group.

Any individual in the right situation can be a sociometric star; that same individual in another group, based on other criteria, can be an isolate or rejectee.

A Sociometric Rejectee is an individual who receives an unexpected number of rejections from the individuals in the group. He/she has no power to influence people within the system. Many times they then use their power to disrupt the process of the group. By doing this they are often one of the most powerful (as in time and attention paid to them) members in the group. One way they may subtly disrupt the group process is by incessantly asking questions. The rejectee has a tremendous amount of power to affect or interrupt the process of the group.

A Sociometric Isolate is an individual that is not chosen on any criterion. He/she neither chooses nor is chosen. People forget they were in the group and can even forget their name. Unlike the rejectee who is constantly rejected by the group members, the isolate is unconsciously rejected. Frequently, people try to hook up two isolates, hoping that then they will both fit. It is more likely that the result of this hook-up will be an isolated dyad.

A person who receives more than the expected number of choices on a given criterion is called the sociometric star. A person that receives more than the expected number of choices on many given criteria is called the sociometric leader. The sociometric leader has the most power to influence the process of the group. They are the person that will incorporate the norms, (what's acceptable) of that group.

The person that has the figurehead is the nominal leader of the group. Nominal leaders may or may not be the sociometric stars also. Often they are appointed to their position yet they do not command the respect, loyalty, or influence to effectively lead the group to high levels of functioning.

Now apply your newly acquired knowledge of sociometry to your own family. What beliefs, attitudes, or behaviors are positively rewarded in your family? What ones are not tolerated or accepted? Which of these make a family member a sociometric star? Which ones make someone a rejectee or isolate? How often do these roles change? Do you want to change the roles in your family? How would you like it to be for yourself and the other members of your family? The information in Chapter 9, *Relationships*, on parents and conflict resolution will be helpful.

Draw a sociogram of your family.

With permission of Dr. Jerie K. Wood, Center for Human Development.

CHANGED CHILDREN AWAIT PARENTS AT THE HOLIDAYS
(Reprint of Radio Interview)

The faces will look familiar, but the personalities will be changed. Parents having their children return home from college for the first time at Thanksgiving or Christmas are in for a shock, according to a Western Michigan University counselor.

The transition from high school to college is the biggest transition these students are ever going to go through in their lives," says Dr. Richard Oxhandler, a Counseling Psychologist in the WMU Counseling Center. "It's hard to imagine that a few months can change somebody, but those first few months at college do."

Students returning home at the holidays are no longer children, according to Dr. Oxhandler. "They're coming home with much more of a sense of autonomy. I think parents will see somebody who is a little more independent. Parents may use different words for that--'you're out of line' or 'you're much more assertive.' "Parents may see more of a willingness on the part of their students to take action in ways they didn't before," continues Dr. Oxhandler. "Perhaps the student will initiate contact with friends when before he or she used to sit and wait for somebody to call. They may take action in terms of taking care of some tasks at home such as rearranging their rooms or contacting some office concerning financial aid matters that they wouldn't have done before without a parent's direction." Parents should react positively when they see their sons and daughters displaying autonomy in such responsible ways. "Parents have expectations of their children, no matter how much they want to say they don't. Some parents still have a basic expectation that their student is going to come home as a child. They're not - and that can be threatening to parents. It's hard on parents to let go of their children, but it's important that they do. If the student is going to develop into a responsible adult who will have a very positive relationship with his or her parents, the parents must let go," says Dr. Oxhandler.

College life is not the total cause of the changes seen in students by their parents. "It's not the fact they've been at college for a couple of months that brings about the changes, " Dr. Oxhandler says. "It's the fact the students have been going through a number of developmental changes for several years and college is the catalyst for bringing out new behaviors and opportunities for students."

In high school, students find themselves in what Dr. Oxhandler terms "a very strong support group". They're in touch with parents, friends, relatives, classmates, teachers, and members of religious groups and other organizations. "When they come to a school like Western, this support group isn't there - at least not the minute they hit campus - and this opens up a whole new realm of possibilities. They need to find out who they truly are as individuals without having those old support groups as a reference point," he says. "It's scary for them and it's exciting for them."

How can parents and students deal with these changes during the holidays? "For one thing, parents must recognize they're dealing now with an adult who is working as best as he or she can to be more of a peer," Dr. Oxhandler says. "Parents will always be in a parent's role, but it's important for them to foster the growth of their child instead of putting them back into the old role of 'dependent child'. Students have to keep in mind that parents have their rights. A student can't come in and say, 'Now, I'm an independent human being and you're just going to have to take me as I am', without understanding that parents might like to get to sleep at 11 p.m. because they have to work the next day. They have to recognize that there's a certain level of noise and certain behaviors that are acceptable and those that are not".

"Keeping lines of communication open is a key to holiday happiness", says Dr. Oxhandler. "Students, when they go away to college, will try a lot of behaviors initially because they've never done them before or to be accepted by their new friends. This may be behavior in areas such as sex, politics, drinking, drugs, or things that parents aren't comfortable with at all. If parents come down real heavy on students for their behavior in a very judgmental way, they close off communication. Parents who work to talk with their son or daughter on an adult-to-adult level will have more success than those who try to control their son's or daughter's behavior by dictating to them on a parent-to-child level. Students will tend to work things through in ways that are healthy for them if they can talk it out and feel they have a safe place to talk. It's nice when parents can supply that place to talk."

Chapter 12 - EPB Mind Stretchers

1. Define acceptance and tolerance.
2. In sociometry the main thing to remember about the rejectee is?
3. Why is acceptance important to your child?
4. What evidence do you have that your, as well as your child's, tolerance and acceptance boundaries have expanded this semester? (Hint: review your EPB worksheets and summary page)
5. What solutions would you offer to resolve family communication problems based on sociometric roles you wish changed?
6. Prioritize (with 1 as the highest) the five people in your life from whom you want to receive the most tolerance and acceptance. Now do likewise for five people to whom you wish to give more tolerance and acceptance. Repeat this for each member of your family.

SUCCESS TRIAD SUMMARY
Chapter 12 - Tolerance and Acceptance

CHALLENGES:

1. Love themselves in a healthy way so no other person, animal, plant, or the environment is diminished or destroyed in order for them to feel superior or as a result of their self-hate.
2. Devote the energy necessary to truly try to understand other's views without prejudging.
3. Be the healthiest mentally, physically, emotionally and spiritually so they have more to give and less to fear.

SUPPORT:

1. Provide the finances for your daughter or son to engage in activities where they learn about and/or interact with peoples from other cultures, religions, economic conditions etc.
2. Provide the finances for your son or daughter to engage in activities that expand their understanding of the natural world, its plant and animal life and their responsibility to protect and preserve our planet.

CARING:

1. Model tolerance and acceptance in your interactions with them, others, and the natural world.
2. Lovingly confront bias, prejudice, cruelty and indifference on the part of your son or daughter and encourage them to be more accepting and loving.
3. Model self-responsibility and social responsibility.

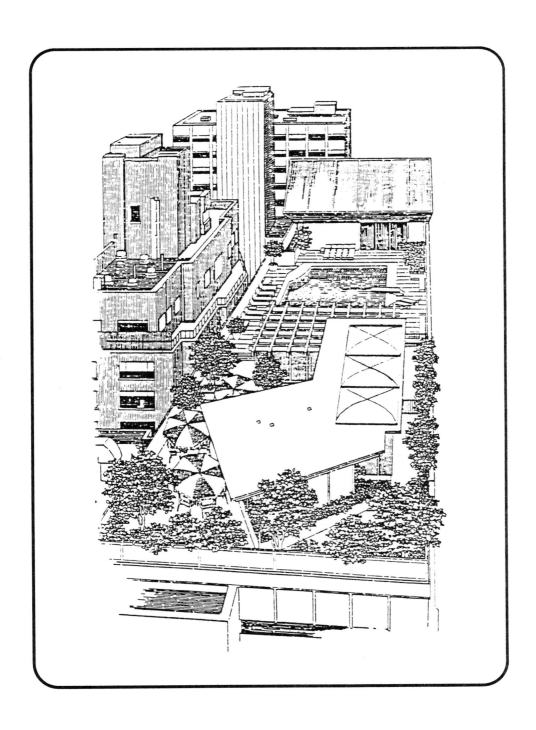

Chapter Thirteen
Kalamazoo

KALAMAZOO

The city of Kalamazoo has many resources available to the knowledgeable student. Not unlike their situation on campus, students who know what resources are available in their city and how and when to use them will find it easier to get their needs met. Whether looking for an auto repair shop, paying a traffic ticket, attending a local concert or sporting event, finding gourmet to fast food restaurants, parks, the bus station, a dentist, or a fine jazz band, they will save time, energy, possibly money, reduce stress and add cultural enrichment and pleasure to their lives if they can use the resources available Kalamazoo.

The phone book, especially the yellow pages, the Chamber of Commerce, daily newspapers and trade papers, telephone information services, the Western <u>Herald</u>, and local television are readily available sources of information about local resources. Another excellent source can be students, faculty, staff and townspeople who have lived in Kalamazoo for some time.

Kalamazoo is a city that for its size is exceptionally rich and diverse. The opportunities available to the resourceful student for fun, enrichment and adventure are nearly unlimited. Encourage your daughter or son to use public transportation, visit the downtown area for shopping, meals, or entertainment, spend time at the planetarium, art gallery, museum, or library. In addition knowing where to get repairs done on the car or a toothache taken care of can do much to alleviate a sense of helplessness and dependency on their part and provide reassurance for you.

The exercise below is to be completed using at least three information sources for the ten resource areas listed below. For example, under restaurant they could put Rex Cafe, 432 S. Burdick, 343-4993, telephone book., You could do this activity together as a family during a visit.

Have fun! Discover Kalamazoo.

Resource	**Information Source**		
	Name	Address	Phone#
Restaurant			
Entertainment			
Recreation			
Services			

176

NOTES

Resource	Information Source		
	Name	Address	Phone#
Hair Styling			
Bank			
Train/Bus Station			
Medical Care			
Housing/ Rental Properties			
Concert Facility			
Dental care			

ASSESSING YOUR GROWTH!

Your college age child has experienced many new people, situations, ideas, and feelings during the past few months. Often so much is happening that it can be difficult for them to determine if, how much, or in what ways they are learning and growing. As a parent who is concerned and cares enough about the growth, success, and happiness of your child that you have read and done the activities in this book, you are in an ideal position to provide feedback about their growth and learning from your perspective.

Please, take the time needed to thoughtfully complete the Risk-Taking in Groups and Life-Space Situations questionnaires found at the end of Chapter 14. To gain the most from this exercise, do not look at the questionnaires you completed a few months ago or your responses on the summary sheets. Covering your first responses with a piece of paper should work fine. Once completed, put the difference in the Change + or - column. (example: if a response changed from 5 to 3 put -2 in the Change column)

In this assessment a change in the - (minus) direction represents an expansion of your child's boundary in that arena. A change in the + (plus) direction represents a contraction of your child's boundary. This can often indicate an increased awareness of a problem previously avoided or a decision to confront it more directly which would (at least temporarily) increase their stress. So a + isn't necessarily a negative.

The vast majority of students have many more responses that indicate they have expanded their boundaries than they would have guessed. So even at the end of their first term of college, it can be difficult for them to accurately assess their growth! After you have reviewed your perceptions of your child's growth, plan a time when you and the family can sit down to celebrate this growth with your son or daughter. Don't be put off by thinking this is silly. Your child will appreciate you taking the time to do all the reading and work necessary to make such observations, they will feel better about themselves since some growth is obvious, and they will feel the caring, support, and love from you that makes so much of the hard work worthwhile. Plan a true celebration of your daughter or son!

Now take a few minutes to appreciate yourself for the effort, discipline, and commitment you put forth in order to support your child and his/her efforts to achieve this growth. Celebrate yourself as a loving and caring parent!

178

Chapter Fourteen
Termination

TERMINATIONS

Terminations of our relationships are a natural and important part of life. They are natural in that all relationships terminate; some terminate when friends move away, some when we choose to end a marriage, others through death. Not all relationship terminations mean we never see the other person again, but they always mean there is a significant change in the way we relate to another person. For example, your daughter might terminate a romantic relationship yet remain friends with her boyfriend.

The termination of a relationship is also important because we are losing someone in a way that was meaningful to us which necessitates going through a time of grieving for our loss. Incomplete terminations, when we didn't say all we needed to say to a person, are important because we often carry this unfinished business into other similar relationships. For example, if you son was never able to tell his roommate how angry he was with the way the room was kept, he will most likely not be able to tell his new roommate when he feels angry with his behavior.

It is easier to move on with our lives and move into more productive relationships when we have taken care of all we need to say and do in our previous relationships. Before you go on in this chapter, review your completed summary sheets at the end of the text. Look over the values, skills and strengths you have identified for your daughter or son. Do you like what you see? Any changes you wish them to make now? Review the changes in your responses on the Risk-Taking in Groups and Life-Space Situations questionnaires from the first to the second time you filled them out. Are you surprised by their growth? Encourage them to keep it up! In four or five years when they graduate the growth they have made will be remarkable.

Now I would like you to do some terminating with your experience relative to this book. Remember how you felt and what you thought of yourself, your son or daughter, your spouse, your other offspring, and WMU after that first visit to campus or after reading the introduction to this book? Have you changed? What have you done to change? In what ways has this book been an aid to your growth and helpful in your efforts to support the success of your son or daughter? What else do you wish had been included in this book or perhaps excluded or changed? What experiences do you value most and least from having gone through the readings and exercises? What will you change for next term for yourself? What changes will you encourage and support in your child? What is the single most important thing you have learned from this book? What are you doing for yourself to be happy, productive and successful? I hope you will share these thoughts and feelings with your college age son or daughter and others important in your life.

182

The information you have discovered and learned to appreciate about your child, yourself, others, and your world will be valuable to you the rest of your life, whether as a parent supporting the growth of a child or an individual working to expand your own boundaries. You have made this book yours and it may now serve you as a familiar and trusted resource.

I thank you for taking the time and putting in the energy and commitment necessary to better understand the needs of your child and to support his or her growth, happiness, and success. My wish is that you will always be willing to risk for what you believe to be in the best interest of your child's growth - that you will continue the exciting adventure of supporting the expansion of their perceptual boundaries, and yours!

RISK-TAKING IN GROUPS SUMMARY SHEET

	First Session	Last Session	Change + or -
1. Disclosing certain negative feelings about myself to others.			
2. Revealing certain things about my past to others.			
3. Asking for help with my problems from others.			
4. Expressing anger toward someone in the group.			
5. Expressing affection toward someone in the group.			
6. Receiving affection from someone in the group.			
7. Asking for feedback from significant members in the group.			
8. Touching someone else in the group.			
9. Having someone else touch me in the group.			
10. Becoming close and personal with another in front of the group.			
11. Making a statement which might anger someone else in the group.			
12. Expressing and dealing with conflict I have with another member in the group.			
13. Giving another member negative feedback.			
14. Being the center of attention in the group.			
15. Expressing my confusion and uncertainty in front of the other group members.			
16. Expressing anger or dissatisfaction with the group leader.			
17. Admitting that I was wrong about some other person in the group.			
18. Admitting to the group that I was wrong about an idea that I had.			

(continued on next page)

	First Session	Last Session	Change + or -
19. Talking about sexual feelings in the group.	19. _____		_____
20. Sharing a fantasy I have about some member or the total group.	20. _____		_____
21. Telling someone in the group that they have become very important to me.	21. _____		_____
22. Expressing indifference toward other group members.	22. _____		_____
23. Expressing feelings about another member's physical characteristics.	23. _____		_____
24. Talking about my feelings with regard to my physical characteristics.	24. _____		_____
25. Admitting that someone had hurt my feelings in the group.	25. _____		_____
26. Telling the group members to leave me alone, to "get off my back".	26. _____		_____
27. Walking out of the group while under stress.	27. _____		_____
28. Expressing sexual attraction toward another member in the group.	28. _____		_____

Total +_____

Total - _____

LIFE-SPACE SITUATIONS SUMMARY SHEET

		First Session	Last Session	Change + or -
1.	Talking in class			
2.	Talking to a professor			
3.	Asking someone for a date			
4.	Confronting a roommate about a problem			
5.	Confronting a boy/girlfriend about a problem			
6.	Talking to strangers at a party			
7.	Taking tests			
8.	Confronting a boss			
9.	Making decisions			
10.	Giving compliments			
11.	Trusting others			
12.	Accepting compliments			
13.	Asking for help			
14.	Writing a paper for class			
15.	Taking midterm or final exams			
16.	Confronting parents			
17.	Saying I love you			
18.	Confronting old friends			
19.	Registering for classes			
20.	Expressing your religious beliefs			
21.	Choosing a career field			
22.	Expressing your anger			
23.	Driving in a big city			
24.	Expressing affection physically			
25.	Participating in a sport you're not very good at			
26.	Visiting the dentist			
27.	Admitting you were wrong			
28.	Showing your competence			
29.	Showing your weakness			
30.	Returning a defective item to the store			
31.	Helping victims at an auto accident site			

(continued on next page)

		First Session	Last Session	Change + or -
32.	Going skydiving	32.		
33.	Receiving a parking ticket	33.		
34.	Getting chewed out by the boss	34.		
35.	Breaking up a relationship	35.		
36.	Making it on your own after graduation	36.		
37.	Behaving in ways your parents would disapprove	37.		
38.	Going for counseling	38.		
39.	Going caving	39.		
40.	Going rockclimbing	40.		
41.	Attending personal growth workshops	41.		
42.	Spending holidays with family	42.		
43.	Paying for college	43.		
44.	Beginning a fitness program	44.		
45.	Applying for a job	45.		
46.	Having a sexual relationship.	46.		
47.	Experimenting with drugs.	47.		
48.	Starting or stopping attending religious services.	48.		

Total +_____

Total - _____

EXPANDING PERCEPTUAL BOUNDARIES
SUMMARY SHEET

The purpose of this summary sheet is to give you a comprehensive snapshot of your son or daughter. Valuable information about his/her values, strengths, and interests will be collected here as you progress through the book.

Values Workshop (page 24)

Personal Values	Career Values
1.	1.
2.	2.
3.	3.
4.	4.
5.	5.

Spending Their Time (page 36-37)

Values	Skills
1.	1.
2.	2.
3.	3.
4.	4.
5.	5.

Personality Strengths (page 37-40)

1.
2.
3.
4.
5.

Dear Parent,

Thank you for taking the time to read, **PARENTS CARRY A FULL CREDIT LOAD, TOO.** I enjoyed writing this book and hope that you enjoyed and benefitted from reading it. To insure that this book is as informative and helpful to parents in the future, your comments and the comments of others would be appreciated.

Would you, please, take a few minutes to reflect on your experiences with the book and write your comments to the following questions. Feel free to add other comments on a separate sheet of paper if sufficient room is not provided below.

1.   What did you like most about **PARENTS CARRY A FULL CREDIT LOAD, TOO**? What was most helpful to you?

2.   What did you like least about this book? What was least helpful to you?

3.   How useful were the Mind Stretchers and Success Triad Summary Sheets at the end of chapters 1-12?

4.   How helpful were the activities in the chapters?

About the Author

Educated at the State University of New York at Binghamton (B.A.), Syracuse University (Ms.Ed.), and Western Michigan University (Ed.D.), Dr. Richard M. Oxhandler has spent his entire professional career working in higher education. Having served as an administrator, teacher, and counselor, he is currently a counseling psychologist in the University Counseling Center, Western Michigan University in Kalamazoo, Michigan.